ARTS AND CRAFTS
of Chester County, Pennsylvania

by Margaret Schiffer

Schiffer Publishing Ltd

Box E, Exton, Pennsylvania 19341

Book Design by Steven Carothers

Library of Congress catalog card number 80-52028

ISBN 0-916838-35-8

Table of Contents

Dedication:

To my Mother, Ellen McMichael Berwind

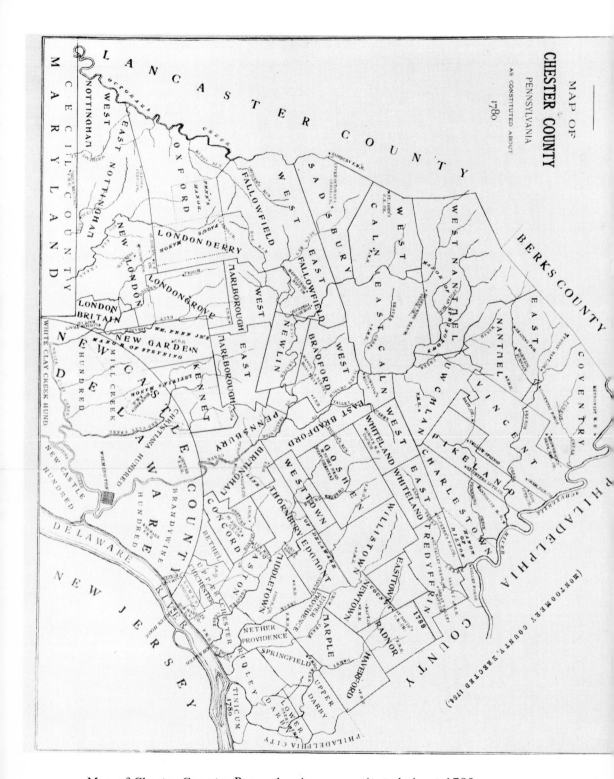

Map of Chester County, Pennsylvania, as constituted about 1780.

From Gilbert Cope, Genealogy of the Smedley Family (Lancaster, Pa. 1901), p. 47. (Photo by Ned Goode)

Introduction

CHESTER COUNTY

Chester County is one of the three original counties formed in 1682 in Pennsylvania by William Penn under Charter signed by King Charles II. Before this time Indians, Dutch, Swedes, Finns and English lived along the Delaware River, the Schuylkill River and tributary creeks in what was to become the southeastern portion of Pennsylvania.

The greatest number of settlers after 1682 came from the British Isles. Many English and Welsh Quakers and Baptists settled here in the 1680's, also Presbyterians and members of the Church of England. The English Quakers settled in the eastern and southeastern townships as well as in the Great Valley. In the first quarter of the eighteenth century there was a migration of Irish Quakers and of Scotch Irish Presbyterians who settled chiefly in the southern and western townships.

Finally, at the end of the first quarter of the eighteenth century the northern tier of townships received many settlers, the so-called Pennsylvania Dutch. A few French and other nationalities also settled within the county.

Men travelling through the county have left us interesting observations.

In 1678 Jasper Dancaerts, a Dutch traveller, described a house in the Delaware Valley.

> Their Houses are Mats, or Bark of Trees set on Poles, in the fashion of an English Barn, but out of the power of the Winds, for they are hardly higher than a Man; they lie on Reeds or Grass. In Travel they lodge in the Woods about a great Fire, with the Mantle of Duffels they wear by day, wrapt about them, and a few Boughs stuck round them.[1]
>
> If an European comes to see them, or calls for Lodging at their House of Wigwam they give him the best place and first cut.[2]

William Penn, in 1682, described the house of the Delaware Indians.

> The house although not much larger than where we spent the last night, was somewhat better and tighter, being made according to the Swedish mode, and as they usually build their houses here, which are blockhouses, or houses of hewn logs being nothing else than entire trees, split through the middle or somewhat squared out of the rough, these trees are laid in the form of a square upon each other as high as they wish to have the house, the ends of these timbers are let into each other, about a foot from the ends of them. So stands

the whole building without nail of spike, the ceiling and the roof do not show much finer work, except among the most particular who also have all the ceilings planked and also a glass window. The doors are wide enough but very low, so that everyone must stoop to enter in, always these houses are tight and warm, but the chimney stands in the corner.[3]

In October 1725 Robert Park, of Chester County, wrote:

DEAR SISTER MARY VALENTINE,
. . .Land is of all Prices Even from ten pounds to one hundred pounds a hundred, according to the goodness or else the Situation thereof, & Grows dearer every year by Reason of Vast Quantities of People that come here yearly from Several Parts of the world, therefore thee & thy family or any that I wish well wod desire to make what Speed you can to come here the Sooner the better we have traveled over a Pretty deal of this country to seek for Land and (tho) we met with many fine Tracts of Land here and there in the country, yet my father being curious & somewhat hard to Please Did not buy any Land until the Second day of the 10th mo: Last and then he bought a Tract of Land consisting of five hundred Acres for which he gave 350 pounds, it is Excellent good land but none cleared, Except about 20 Acres, with a small log house & Orchard Planted, We are going to clear some of it Directly, for our next Sumers fallow, we might have bought Land much cheaper but not so much to our satisfaction. We stayed in Chester 3 months & then Rented a Place 1 mile from Chester, with a good brick house & 200 Acres of Land for (?) pounds a year where we continue till next May.[4]

Peter Kalm, a Swedish naturalist travelling in the Delaware Valley between 1748 and 1751 observed:

About two English miles behind Chester I passed by an iron forge, which was to the right hand by the road side. It belonged to two brothers, as I was told. The ore, however, is not dug here, but thirty or forty miles from hence, where it is first melted in the oven, and then carried to this place. The bellows were made of leather, and both they and the hammers, and even the hearth (were) but small in proportion to ours. All the machines were worked by water. The iron was wrought into bars.[5]

Doctor Alexander Hamilton, in 1774, visits Chester and Darby.

We passed thro' Chester at seven o'clock at night, where we left Morison, Smith, and Howard; and the parson and I jogged on intending to reach Darby, a town about nine or ten miles from Chester.
    Chester is a pretty neat and large village. Built chiefly of brick, pleasantly situated upon a small river of the same name that discharged itself into Delaware, about half a mile below where the village stands. Over this river is a wooden bridge, built with large rafters and planks in form of an arch. The State-house is a pretty enough building; this put me in mind of Chelsea near London, which it resembles for neatness, but it is not so large.
    The parson and I arrived at Darby, our resting place, at half an hour after eight at night. This village stands in a bottom and partly upon the ascent of a hill, which makes it have a dull, melancholy appearance. We put up at a publick house kept by one Thomas, where the landlady looked after everything herself, the land lord being drunk as a lord. The liquor had a very strange effect upon him, having deprived him of the use of his tongue. He sat motionless in a corner, smoking his pipe and would have made a pretty good figure upon arras.

We were entertained with an elegant dispute between a young Quaker and the boatswain of a privateer, concerning the lawfulness of using arms against an enemy. The Quaker thee'd and thou'd the nose to perfection, and the privateer's boatswain swore just like the boatswain of a privateer, but they were so far from settling the point that the Quaker had almost acted contrary to his principles, clenching his fist at his antagonist to strike him for bidding God damn him. At nine Mr. Usher and I went to bed.[6]

In 1787 Samuel Vaughan observed that:

From Philadelphia to the Susquehannah the farmers are for the most part German and many publick houses on the road, the English Soldiers often at time stood in need of a Linguist, but on crossing the River there are many Irish who are neither so industrious, sober, or well informed in farming as the Germans who are the most valuable settlers.[7]

Johann David Schoeph travelling in the confederation between 1783 and 1784 mentions:

On the low hills to the west of the river [Schuylkill], made up likewise of limestone rock, loose quartz, fragments are found in great quantity, frequently set off with fine crystals. These occur especially on Mr. Rambo's land, which is throughout based on the limestone. This observation, that crystals are very generally, if not always, found on limestone soil, I have confirmed, in many other parts of America.

The Schuylkill is here commonly not so deep but one may ride through . . .

Between Swedes-Ford and Valley Forge there are to be seen many pits for burning lime; but on the surface along that road only common quartz and sandstone. The height, at the foot of which lies Valley-Forge, was over strewn with a quantity of hard, slatey, sandstones, in which here and there appeared little blackish points of what seemed to be shorl. The opposite hill consisted almost entirely of a brown rotten iron-ore mixed with mica . . . The works and buildings at the forge were burned down during the war. The ore which was smelted and worked here comes from a valley near-by.

The hills, over which the road lay from here, still seemed to be made up for the most part of a brown iron-mould, or of an earth similar to this. In one of the valleys there was limestone. But this whole region, far around, cannot boast of any particularly fertile soil; but little grain is raised, and there is a lack of meadows, the narrow low grounds along the Schuylkill excepted, which is the sole good land of the region. But the country is so much the more productive in iron-ore, which has been the occasion of setting up a good many forges and furnaces. The forests are everywhere thin and of young growth; for what with the lack of a systematic forest-economy here, the many iron-works could not but ravage the woods, and to their own hurt. The better land is used for farming and the worse, where timber is left standing, produces a slow and poor growth. Moreover the game which at one time was plentiful in the region has in great part been frightened off . . . The people who live in and among these hills seem not to be the most prosperous and their dwellings are not the best. But are not forgotten in the tax-levies; an ordinary house e.g., with 100 acres of land, paid this year 20 Pd. Pensylv. Current. The owner, a German . . .

Coventry, another forge 15 miles from Valley-Forge, belongs to a Mr. Pott. On the road thither iron-mould is still to be seen, at times soft, at times hard, and divers other species of rock, scaly sound-stones, quartz and breccia cemented with sand and iron; and a gneissic rock especially. The forge at Coventry stands in a narrow valley, running east and west. There are three hearths and three hammers. The hammers lie parallel with the shaft, the trunnions of which catch the halve at a little distance behind the hammer, and thus raise it with less power.

The bellows are of wood, and consist of two cylindrical casks, fitting closely the one into the other, and moving up and down between four wooden posts. The wind goes first through a leathern conduit, into an iron pipe, and so to the hearth. These simple bellows have the advantage that they may be set up without trouble or expense, need few repairs, and shold last well. The best bar-iron is at this time sold here at 38 shillings Pensyl. Current the hundredweight, or about 5 pence the pound. Here, as everywhere, the assertion is made that American iron is in no way inferior to the best European . . .

Five miles farther, over barren, stony, woody, and hills, we come to Warwick Mine-holes, which in the district, are very famous iron-mines.[8]

Seven years later, in 1794, Theopile Cazenove mentions in his journal:

November 14th, left McClahan's Tavern, through part of Lancaster [County], still fine land and beautiful meadows, 2 miles; then entered Chester County where for 10 miles the land is less level, more broken by very high hills, generally "barren land," but afterwards you go down in the valley and arrive at

Downing's Town [Downingtown], Chester County, 16-½ miles; stopped at Downing's, at the sign of Washington, a very good inn. N.B. 33 miles from Philadelphia.

In this county, farms are generally about 300 acres, half of which remains as woods — generally lime-stone; a farm with house and good barn, orchard, etc. sells for £12 [per acre] in the valley, and the price of land on the mountain, bordering the valley, called "hill-land," sells for £3, and is kept by the farmers for woodland for their farm use. Generally everything is grain-land or sown in clover, when they give it a rest. They fertilize their soil with lime, taken from their land, and with plaster of Paris; this latter gives a good yield of hay. barn, orchard, etc., sells for £3 and is kept by the farmers for wood-land for their farm use. Generally everything is grain-land or sown in clover, when they give it a rest. They fertilize their soil with lime, taken from their land, and with plaster of Paris; this latter gives a good yield of hay.

An acre in the good valley land generally yields 15 to 20 bushels of wheat, but these last 2 or 3 years they have been annoyed in this district by the Hessian fly and this year (1794) by mildew — so they cultivate corn more extensively, and sow their fields in clover, because when there is not enough wheat sown, the Hessian fly attacks barley; 30 to 35 bushels corn [per acre], 20 to 25 bushels barley, 1-½ to 2 or 2-½ tons of clover in 2 cuttings.

Send their flour and produce to Philadelphia — many mills, a few forges near the mountain, where there is plenty of wood, but no mines.

Every house and barn is built of limestone, no brick-factories. The quality of land in Chester County is quite varied; the country is crossed in the north and south by 2 rows of mountains, not very high, but too high to be estimated of great value for cultivation. The land of the south mountains (chestnut) £3 an acre. The land of the north mountains, generally oak, for £3 an acre.

The land south of the mountains is fair, and is worth £7 to £8 an acre, for 2 or 300 acre farms. The wood on the south mountains chiefly chestnut.

The valley where the land is level and "lime-stone." Farms with improvements, that is to say in activity [?] and in ½ cultivation, are worth £12 an acre.

The land in the north, beyond the mountains is slit-stone, stony, but good for grain, is worth from £5 to £6 an acre for 2 to 400 acre farms. N.B. The trees on the north mountains are generally oak.

November 15th, left Downings T. [Downingtown], passing through a country partly level, partly broken with hills near . . . [arrived] at . . . Fornistak's Tavern, 10 miles, rather bad lodging, on the highway . . . [9]

Thomas Fairfax, in 1799, traveling from Virginia to Salem, Massachusetts passes through Chester County:

Thence 10 miles to DOWNINGTOWN, and the 7 miles to a stone bridge over the west branch of BRANDYWINE. Here there was a Tavern at which the Stage going to LANCASTER, and myself, arrived together. I took this opportunity to relieve my horse in some measure by putting my trunk in the stage, to be left at LANCASTER. I then spoke for dinner and after waiting an hour, sat down to one of the most wretched meals that ever was served on a table. I was never more surprised, for from the appearance of the house, I expected to get something tolerable. I observed the kind of deception to be Common in this Country. You will see before you a large and handsome stone house, with a well painted sign and when you are taken with the bait, and go in, you find nothing but dirt, and the worst Accomodations. From hence I drove 12 miles to the SIGN OF PRESIDENT ADAMS and there lodged. At this house I had ample amends for my illfare at the other, as every thing here was in the best order. Several Travelers had stopped for the night, and we spent an agreeable evening. The 25th early in the morning I left this and drove 5 miles to Breakfast at the SIGN OF THE SPREAD EAGLE, a German house. This is one of the handsome looking stone houses; however, there was no deception, for it was as fair within as without, and well provided. From hence it is 9 miles to LANCASTER.

Very few Germans in this county, except in the 3 townships Spikland [Pikeland], Vincent, and Coventry. English Presbyterians and Quakers prevail in this county, also many Anabaptists in the 3 above townships.

The price for transportation from here to Philadelphia is 15 to 18 pence a 100 pounds, and 2s /6 for a barrel of flour.

You find very easy in this district workmen to help with harvest for 3 s a day, with meals and a pint of whiskey. [10]

In 1806 Robert Sutcliff visited a farm in the Great Valley.

This farm was in a good state of cultivation, with an excellent house, a very large barn, and stabling for many horses, with other conveniences on an extensive scale. The spring house, or dairy, in particular struck my attention, having a trench of spring water, about 2 feet wide and 4 or 5 inches deep, running all around the room, paved at the bottom, and enclosed at the sides with slabs of white marble.

I have before observed, that in the spring water which surrounds the floor of the dairies in this country, are placed the vessels containing the milk &c. and all is thus preserved sweet and cool, in the hottest part of the summer. Another convenience I noticed in this farm-yard, was an appendage to the hog-sty, being a vault, near which was a stream of water, all within the enclosure wherein the hogs were confined. The advantages and comfort thus resulting to these animals, in hot weather must be obvious. On this farm, was an excellent orchard of several acres, the trees of which were at this time in their prime, and now in full bearing, and having been planted by the late Governor Mifflin, whose residence was here, they were well selected. Such abundance of fine fruit I never before beheld, in the same compass of ground; two or three of the best trees were literally broken down with the weight of the fruit. The rent G. A. proposed for his farm, with all these appendages, was about 20 s per acre: and, the quantity being short of 100 acres. The rent would amount to little more than the legal interest for the money which had been expended in buildings. As it was not more than an hour's ride from Philadelphia, and the land of good quality, I thought the price very reasonable. [11]

John Pearson, in 1821:

. . . Crossed the Welsh mountain, and came into a valley abounding with well cultivated farms, the inhabitants mostly Dutch; stopped at a store where an election was going on, the people were all as still mice, and democratic was the order of the day . . . Slept at the second sign of General Green; the landlord had land to sell: at least the sheriff would take the trouble off his hands, and sell it for him. Land had been worth 70 to 80 dollars, but now would fetch but 20 per acre. (55th day) — Passed Downingtown. White wine dearer than in England. I travelled the old Chester road, which is both pleasanter and cheaper than the new road; the waggoners gave me this hint.[12]

. . . . this brought me to Little Brandy Wine . . . Here were plenty of farms to sell cheap, with stone houses, stone barns, and stone spring houses, but an Englishman whom I met, advised me not to make any purchase for the first year, he knew plenty then in Brandy Wine township, but he believed it was a wrong time to make purchase . . . In the cool of the evening we moved on to a tavern five miles off; we were charged high for every thing. Married and single are accomodated in one bed-room, and as for certain utensils which are generally found under Englishmen's beds, and a certain description of small buildings, they are by no means common after you leave Philadelphia . . . [13]

His Highness, Bernhard, Duke of Saxe-Weimar Eisenach mentioned in "Travels Through North America During the Years 1825 and 1826":

[Through Chester County] The whole country is cultivated in a most excellent manner, and covered with handsome farms, many barns look like large churches. [14]

Mrs. Anne Royall, in 1825, described West Chester:

As the distance was short, and I had heard so much of the beauty of the country, and the superior manners, wealth and intelligence of the inhabitants of West Chester, a small town south of Philadelphia,

I took a jaunt to that place. The road from Philadelphia to West Chester passes through one of the handsomest countries I have seen in my travels. As to wealth, fertility and cultivation, it excels. The farms are large and neat; the houses are built of stone principally, not very large, but remarkable for having small windows, their barns and stables are large, comfortable, close and costly. There is nothing like the barns, clover fields and cattle of Pennsylvania to be seen in any State. The whole country is chequered with fields of the rankest red clover. These were on each side of the road and in them stood droves of overgrown, sleek horses and cattle, gorged with clover, which was up to their knees. They were standing still, panting with their own weight. This is the case to West Chester, the twenty-eight miles.

I knew not which to admire most, the appearance of the country, or the neat plump Quaker and his wife, sitting side by side in their tight, comfortable, covered dearborn, going to the Philadelphia market. We met numbers of them in the course of the ride. They seemed to be the happiest people on earth, health on their cheeks, contentment on their countenance. Their white pails of butter sitting at their feet-richly and plainly dressed-their horse trembling with fat, secure from the sun and rain, they were enviable.

West Chester is a most delectable spot, near the Brandywine. It stands in the midst of a fertile country upon an even plain and is inhabited by the first people of the State. I found more taste, talent and refinement in West Chester, in proportion of the number of inhabitants than in any town, without exception, I have visited.***The citizens have built three meeting houses (one belongs to the Friends), and any parson of any sect has the privilege of preaching as often as he pleases, but not one cent of money does he receive. The citizens have entered into resolutions never to pay one cent of money to any priest.

See West Chester — let any man visit that town he will find it possessed of more virtue, hospitality, charity and intelligence than any town he has ever been in.

But West Chester speaks for itself. I never enjoyed myself more in any town. It is a perfect treat. They have a large collection (for the time) of choice books, minerals and a variety of productions of the terraqueous globe, all scientifically arrayed. This is the work of Dr. Darlington one of the most, if not altogether the most scientific man in the State of Pennsylvania. I was particularly struck with his cool, keen, steady penetrating eye.

They also have an athenaeum tastefully selected, and appear to be taking the lead in improving society. They seem to be aware of true happiness in the first place, and in the second place, they are in the right road to obtain it. There appears to be a harmony and mutual ambition for science and improvement, which can be met with in no other place. I had but a piece of day to spend there, which I deeply lamented, but I trust to spend some pleasant hours yet with those enviable people. I never was in a place where I saw less foppers. I believe it as clear of dandies as parsons . . . [15]

Charles B. Trego in "A Geography of Pennsylvania" in 1843 observed:

The traveller in the older settled parts of Pennsylvania is particularly struck with the neat and substantial appearance of the buildings, fences, &c. as well as the order and convenience of the whole domestic arrangement of a well regulated farm. The pride of a Pennsylvania farmer is his barn, many of which are from 60 to 120 feet in length and substantially built, either wholly of stone, or the lower story of stone and the superstructure of wood, handsomely painted or whitewashed. The interior arrangement of stables, threshing floor, granaries, places for depositing hay, &c., is admirably convenient and useful. The horses, cattle and other domestic animals are comfortably sheltered during the winter, and like their master and family, enjoy the plenty provided by good husbandry and provident industry.[16]

In 1854 a country gentleman writes:

In passing from Philadelphia to Lancaster, the first twenty-five miles presented nothing very notable, except what may be seen in all parts of the country settled by the Dutch. The farm houses are not large, or of tasty design, but the barns are large, substantial, and the commodious structures, well calculated as storehouses for grain, and to afford comfortable shelter for the cattle. Many of them are built of stone, and they as well as other farm buildings, are mostly white washed externally and look clean and healthy.[17]

From the 1680's until after the Centennial celebration of 1876 the rest of Chester county, due to its fertile soil and temperate climate, had chiefly an agricultural dairying economy. The most important crop was wheat. Grain and flour were sold by the inhabitants of the county in Philadelphia and Wilmington. Many early mills, principally for flour and lumber, were built along the Brandywine, Elk, Octorara, Pickering, Valley, French and Pigeon creeks. Each section had a host of craftsmen whose products were chiefly for local consumption.

The first United States Federal Census was taken in 1790 just one year after Delaware county was formed from the southeastern part of Chester county. This census shows a total of four thousand four hundred and fifty-four families comprising 27,939 individuals. The rapid growth of the population of the county is reflected in the following figures from the Federal Census: 1800, 32,093; 1810, 39,597; 1820, 44,451; 1830, 50,910; 1840, 57,515 and in 1850, 66,438. By 1900 the population had increased to 96,628. Since the end of World War II, many areas of the county have become building developments, homes for employees in the industrial centers of Philadelphia, Chester and Wilmington. The 1960 Census listed 207,746 people and the 1970 Census 277,746 people living in Chester county.

Trades, occupations, professions and businesses are not regularly indicated in the tax assessment transcripts until 1796, but starting in the seventeenth century there is an occasional mention of them. The following list has been compiled from available Chester county tax assessments, wills, deeds, mortgages and inventories. The terminology is that actually used in the original record.

A study of the tax lists, wills, deeds, mortgages and other official documents give the following occupations and dates when first listed:

BEFORE 1700
Attorney 1699
Boat wright 1682
Brick layer 1696
Carpenter 1677
Cooper 1699
Cordwainer 1692
Doctor 1678
Glover 1691
House carpenter 1695
Husbandman 1678
Joiner 1691
Linen weaver 1690
Malster 1693
Mariner 1678
Mason 1697
Merchant 1679
Miller 1697
Plow wright 1697
Ship wright 1698
Shoemaker 1699
Silversmith 1696
Smith 1693
Surgeon 1682
Tailor 1677
Turner 1697
Weaver 1690
Webster 1688
Wool seed comber 1694
Worsted comber 1694

1700 THROUGH 1724
Baker 1700
Brick maker 1705
Blacksmith 1704
Clerk 1720
Clothier 1723
Felt maker 1713
Ffashon 1711
Glazier 1719
Hatter 1712
Inn keeper 1712
Mercer 1709
Mill wright 1705
Practioner of Physick 1718
Sadler 1720
Sawyer 1708
Stocking weaver 1716
Surveyor 1700
Tanner 1717
Tin plate worker 1712
Waterman 1724
Wheelwright 1702
Wool comber 1715

1725 THROUGH 1749
Bookbinder 1734

Cloth maker 1736
Currier 1729
Cutler 1747
Finer 1747
Fuller 1730
Hosier 1737
Iron monger 1725
Iron works 1737
Lawyer 1738
Scrivener 1749
Ship carpenter 1743
Store keeper 1740
Tinker 1739

1750 THROUGH 1799
Apothecary 1764
Barber 1768
Barrister 1770
Basket maker 1764
Blade miller 1764
Boatman 1770
Brass founder 1764
Brewer 1764
Butcher 1764
Carter 1764
Cart wright 1764
Chairmaker 1764
Chapman 1759
Clockmaker 1768
Clockman 1770
Cloth worker 1761
Cobbler 1762
Collier 1751
Comb maker 1768
Coppersmith 1768
Corn miller 1770
Dealer 1773
Dish turner 1779
Distiller 1763
Ditcher 1766
Doctor of physick 1761
Drawering 1767
Drover 1772
Farmer 1751
Farrier 1768
Ferrying 1764
Fisher 1766
Flour dealer 1768
Forge 1758
Forgeman 1770
Gardener 1764
Grist miller 1764
Gunsmith 1770
Hemp miller 1764
Hostler 1766
Housekeeper 1768

Iron 1764
Iron master 1740
Jobber 1764
Jockey 1767
Leather milling 1766
Lime burner 1767
Lime pedlar 1764
Long shoreing 1771
Master 1768
Meal dealer 1768
Merchant miller 1764
Miner 1756
Minister 1762
Nailor 1756
Needleman 1766
Nurseyman 1768
Oil miller 1764
Painter 1759
Paper maker 1751
Paper milling 1764
Pedlar 1759
Physician 1774
Plasterer 1769
Plate milling 1773
Plow maker 1766
Pot ash maker 1764
Potter 1764
Quarryman 1764
Reed maker 1768
Ring spigget 1770
Rope maker 1764
Saddle tree maker 1764
Saw miller 1764
School master 1764
School teacher 1759
Screen maker 1770
Scythe maker 1767
Sea man 1772
Shallopman 1757
Ship joiner 1768
Ship wright 1764
Shop joiner 1761
Shop keeping 1753
Sieve maker 1771
Skin dresser 1753
Skinner 1758
Spinning mill 1759
Spinning wheel maker 1768
Stave maker 1759
Stove maker 1768
Tavern keeper 1759
Thatcher 1766
Tin man 1764
Tub milling 1774
Vendue crying 1768

Veterinarian 1771
Wagoner 1770
Watchmaker 1764
Waterman 1767
Wheel maker 1768
Whetstone maker 1764
Whitesmith 1766
Wire weaving 1772

1800 THROUGH 1824

Accountant 1818
Apple tree maker 1803
Architect 1817
Bar keeper 1804
Bark house 1808
Bell maker 1809
Book keeper 1803
Book seller 1818
Boot maker 1814
Broom maker 1807
Cake baker 1812
Cake seller 1807
Cake wife 1813
Calling 1809
Card machine 1807
Carder 1814
Carding factory 1818
Carding mill 1814
Cashier 1815
Chaffery 1813
Chafing & finery forge 1814
Cheese maker 1807
Chopping mill 1823
Cidar mill house 1811
Clergyman 1805
Cloth manufactory 1817
Clover mill 1808
Clover seed works 1818
Coach trimmer 1819
Coal burner 1816
Coal house 1800
Coaler 1804
Confectionary 1824
Cotton reader 1822
Cotton spinner 1819
Cropper 1819
Collector of Internal tax 1814
Copper plate worker 1821
Corder 1818
Cording machine 1808
Cordwood cutter 1808
Cotton factory 1811
County gate keeper 1812
County merchant 1813
Court crier 1806
Dentist 1824
Diaper weaver 1809

Druggist 1806
Drummer 1819
Drying house 1801
Dryer 1803
Dyer 1807
Editor 1813
Factory 1812
Factory mills 1819
Fan maker 1809
Finery forge 1816
Flax dresser 1809
Flour merchant 1815
Forge clerk 1813
Forge hammerman 1811
Frame net worker 1811
Framework knitter 1810
Fruit vender 1809
Funnel 1819
Furnace man 1801
Gimblet maker 1815
Granary 1811
Grog drinker 1811
Gun factory 1823
Gun powder manufactory 1814
Hair dresser 1809
Hair weaver 1809
Hammersmith 1816
Harness maker 1819
Horse dealer 1810
Horse trader 1809
House jointer 1800
House turnpike keeper 1806
Iron merchant 1813
Iron slitter 1805
Knitter 1808
Ladies hair dresser 1807
Ladle maker 1804
Latin master 1807
Leather house 1805
Lamp black house 1818
Lamp black, ink power & printer
    Ink maker 1814
Legislator 1818
Lime kiln 1803
Lime stone quarry 1809
Lime stone quarry & kiln 1803
Livery stable 1817
Locksmith 1812
Lumber merchant 1820
Manager 1801
Mantua maker 1813
Manufacturer 1814
M. D. 1806
Magistrate 1812
Mail stage driver 1815
Mechanic 1804

Mill wright 1801
Mine raiser 1809
Minister of the Peace 1810
Missionary 1810
Money lender 1822
Nail factory 1803
Nail header 1811
Nail shop 1811
Office 1824
Oil maker 1801
Oiler 1803
Ostler 1819
Ore bank 1803
Overseer 1801
Oysterman 1823
P. M. 1812
P maker 1818
Pastor 1813
Plaster mill 1803
Plaster works 1813
Platter works 1811
Post & railer 1808
Post carrier 1822
Post fence maker 1806
Post master 1814
Pot house 1803
Pot moulder 1803
Pottery 1818
Powder maker 1801
Preacher of the gospel 1807
Printing shop 1811
Professor 1817
Pump borer 1801
Quarry 1806
Reader 1822
Recorder 1814
Register 1814
Roller 1807
Rolling mill 1805
Schooler 1815
School keeper 1819
Sea faring 1801
Shingle manufacturer 1803
Ship 1810
Shop 1809
Shop carpenter 1806
Shop keeper 1813
Sickle maker 1805
Slaughter house 1820
Spinner 1814
Spinning machine 1811
Stage 1814
Stage driver 1800
Stage keeper 1807
Steel founder 1812
Steel refiner 1800

Still 1809
Stock taker 1808
Stone breaker 1811
Stone cutter 1811
Stone mason 1806
Store 1819
Store tender 1803
Student 1809
Student at law 1818
Student in medicine 1811
Student in physick 1800
Stumping mill 1818
Sute maker 1811
Sutler 1808
Teacher 1809
Teacher of languages 1824
Thorn weaver 1805

Tilt forge 1803
Tilt hammersmith 1801
Tilt man 1807
Tilt mill 1803
Tilt works 1800
Tin maker 1809
Tin manufactory 1802
Tinner 1824
Tin worker 1804
Tinker 1821
Treasurer 1822
Tiplen shop 1812
Trip hammer 1814
Trunk maker 1807
Undertaker 1816
V. D. M. 1814
Victualler 1812

Vine dresser merchant 1803
Viver 1805
W. W. 1816
Waister 1822
Waiter 1812
Warehouse 1809
Weaving factory 1823
Well mason 1820
Whiskey seller 1811
Wood hauler 1803
Wool carder 1806
Wool factory 1816
Wool house 1805
Woolen manufactory 1816
Wright 1813

In the 1796 tax assessments the following numbers of men are listed with an occupation: 210 weavers; 118 blacksmiths; 116 saw millers; 104 carpenters; 94 masons; 84 grist mills; 70 cordwainers; 68 coopers and shoemakers; 66 tavern keepers; 62 smiths; 60 shop keepers; 59 tanners, 58 tailors; 42 distillers; 35 millers; 31 men working in iron; 26 jobbing; 23 fullers; 23 hatters and 23 joiners; 22 merchant millers and 22 saddle makers; 21 paper makers; 19 doctors; 9 brewers and 9 colliers; 8 wagon makers; 7 cabinet-makers; 7 cart makers; 7 potteries and 7 wheelmakers; 6 oil mills; 5 carters, 5 chairmakers; 5 clockmakers; 5 lime workers and 5 spinning wheel makers; 4 attorneys; 4 hammerers; 4 millwrights; 4 miners; 4 tilt hammerers and 4 watch makers; 3 curriers; 3 pump makers and 3 slit millers; 2 back mills; 2 blue dyers; 2 brick layers; 2 butchers; 2 nurseries; 2 painters; 2 plasterers; 2 reed makers; 2 saddle tree makers; 2 sawyers; 2 tutors; 2 vendue criers and 2 wagoners; 1 brick maker, cidar maker, clothier, conveyancer, cutler, drover, gate keeper, grazier, hosier, hostler, plow maker, shingle maker, stocking weaver and stock taker.

The 1798 Direct Tax gives a vivid picture of the number of buildings in the county.

Apple kiln 4
Bake house 5
Bar 1
Bark mill 7
Barn
   Brick 2
   Frame 204
   Log 596
   Log & frame 19
   Log & stone 74
   Mud 2
   No material specified 41

Stone 292
Stone & frame 33
Stone & wood 12
Wood 63

Barrack 3
Bath house 1
Beam house 5
Blade mill 2
Calf house 1
Cart house 18
Chair house 28
Cheese house 3

Cider house 7
Coal house 7
Corn crib 2
Cow house 16
Distillery 9
Drying house 1
Farm house 1
Forge 4
Fulling mill 13
Garden house 1
Gear house 7
Granary 33

Grist mill 7
Hay house 69
Hog house 2
House
  Brick 182
  Brick & frame 6
  Brick & plank 1
  Frame 144
  Log 1153
  Log hewn 10
  Log round 32
  Log sawed 2
  Log & boarded 2
  Mud 6
  Plank 14
  Rough case 2
  Slab 2
  Stone 936
  Stone & brick 27
  Stone, brick & frame 2
  Stone & frame 17

Stone & log 55
Stone, log & frame 1
Stone & timber 3
Stone & wood 12
Timber 7
Wood 63
Hovel 1
Ice house 5
Kiln 1
Malt house 6
Milk house 146
Mill 9
Oat house 1
Oil mill 3
Out house 9
Paper mill 5
Pot house 3
Powder mill 1
Poultry house 1
Pump house 1
Saddle house 1

Saw mill 29
Shed 66
Shop 218
Slaughter house 4
Smoke house 53
Snuff mill 4
Spring house 712
Stable 460
Still 19
Store house 17
Summer house 2
Tan house 5
Tilt mill 6
Turning mill 5
Vat house 2
Wagon house 103
Wash house 42
Waste house 1
Well house 4
Wood house 6

[1] Myers, Albert Cook, *William Penn His Account of the Lenni Lenape or Delaware Indians 1683,* (Moylan, Pa., 1937), p. 31.

[2] Ibid., p. 32

[3] Eberlain, Harold Donaldson and Hubbard, Cortlandt V. D., *Historic Houses and Buildings of Delaware,* (Dover, Delaware, 1963), p. 5.

[4] Myers, Albert Cook, *Immigration of the Irish Quakers into Pennsylvania 1683-1750 with their Early History in Ireland,* (Swarthmore, Pa.), p. 70.

[5] Benson, Adolph B., editor, *Peter Kalm's Travels in North America,* (New York, N. Y., 1937), Vol. 1, p. 236.

[6] Hamilton, Alexander, *Hamilton's Itinerarium Being a Narrative of a Journey . . . 1744,* (St. Louis, Missouri, 1907), p. 18.

[7] Williams, Edward G., editor, *Samuel Vaughan's Journey or Minutes Made by S. V., From Stage to Stage, on a Tour to Fort Pitt,* (The Western Pennsylvania Historical Magazine #194), p. 63.

[8] Schoeph, Johann David, *Travels in the Confederation 1783-1784,* (Phila., Pa., 1911), p. 3.

[9] Kelsey, Rayner Wickersham, editor, *Cazenove Journal 1794 a Record of the Journey of Theopile Cazenove Through New Jersey and Pennsylvania,* (Haverford, Pa., 1933), p. 78.

[10] Fairfax, Thomas, *Journal from Virginia to Salem, Massachusetts,* (London, England, 1936), p. 26.

[11] Sutcliff, Robert, *Travels in Some Parts of North America in the Years 1804, 1805 & 1806,* (Phila., Pa., 1812), pp. 290,291.

[12] Pearson, John, *Notes Made During a Journey in 1821 in the United States of America,* (London, England, 1822), p. 59.

[13] Ibid., p. 9.

[14] Shoemaker, Alfred L., *Pennsylvania Barn,* (Lancaster, Pa., 1955), p. 16.

[15] *Daily Local News,* (West Chester, Pa.), no date, 1905.

[16] Shoemaker, Alfred L., *Pennsylvania Barn,* (Lancaster, Pa., 1955), p. 17.

[17] Ibid., p. 9.

Chester County Architecture

Brinton 1704 House, Birmingham Township

Basement Kitchen.

Collins Mansion, West Goshen Township, 1727.

Mary Rogers' House, West Goshen Township, 1807.

Residence of W. Ebbs

From the "Map of the Borough of Westchester Chester Co Pa. Survey & Drawn by Martin & Kennedy" 1856.

Loch Aerie, East Whiteland Township Built 1865, Architect, Addison Hutton.

Cedarcroft, East Marlboro Township, 1859.

Quilting at Westtown, ca. 1890-1900.
Chester County Historical Society collection

Hand blocked coverlet, eighteenth-century.
Chester County Historical Society collection

Coverlet marked "associators". In 1748 groups of militia were formed in Chester County due to the fear of the French and Indian attacks resulting from the war declared between the English and the French in 1744.

Chester County Historical Society collection

Woven coverlet marked "I M C Windle 1841 C Peterman Brandywine C C Pa". Casper Peterman was born in the Duchy of Wirtenburg, Germany. In 1806, age 37 years, a weaver by trade he emigrated from Amsterdam to Philadelphia and declared his intention of becoming a citizen and making Chester county his home.

Chester County Historical Society collection

Woven coverlet marked "John Agner W. Grove 1842".

Mr. and Mrs. Alfred Clegg collection

Patchwork authograph quilt made by Isabelle P. Lukens. Under the house is written "Primitive Hall Built in 1738 by Joseph Pennock West Marlboro Chester county". Squares dated 1842 and 1843.
Chester County Historical Society collection

Woven coverlet marked "William S. Freeman 1845 Brandywine C C
Pa".

Mr. and Mrs. Alfred Clegg collection

Victorian patch work quilt.

Chester County Historical Society collection

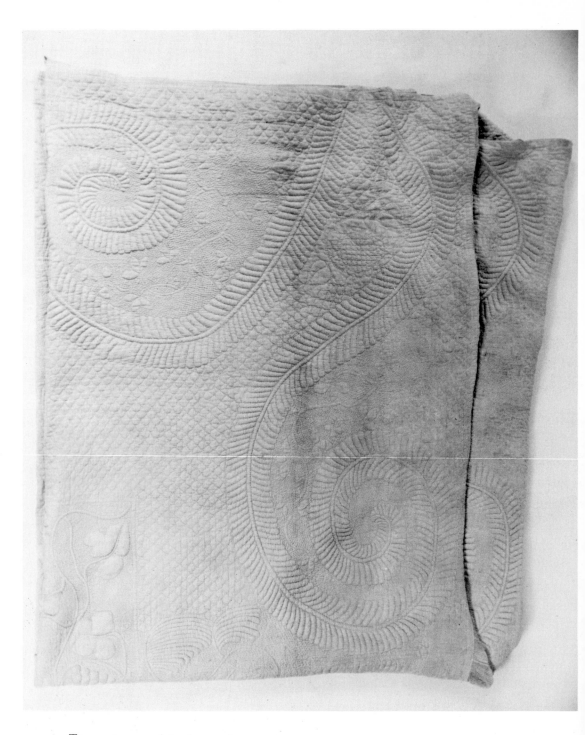

Trapunto work bed covering.
Chester County Historical Society collection

Ceramics

EARTHENWARE

Pottery is an omnibus word which is used to describe everything which is not porcelain. Earthenware is an opaque ware which is porous after the first firing, and which must be glazed before it can be applied to domestic use.

The inventories taken at the time of a person's death, during the seventeenth century mention treen, pewter and earthenware for table use. In the eighteenth century delftware, pewter and earthenware and in the nineteenth century Queensware becomes popular.

Redware, stoneware, brownware, Rockingham ware and yellowware are the various types made by the local potters.

The majority of the potteries were working between 1750 and the time of the Civil War and the period of industrialization. Most of the early potteries were operated on a part time basis. The men were farmers or tradesmen as well as "Bluebird potters". Some of the families engaged in the business continued working for several generations.

Before 1850 the following individual potteries were working in the county.

Paul Benner Pottery
Mahlon Brosius Pottery
Edwin Brosius Pottery
Brown's Pottery
Levi Coates Pottery
Darlington Cope Pottery
Joel Davis Pottery
James Donnelly, West Chester Pottery
Esbin Pottery
Francis Pottery
James Grier, Mount Jordan Pottery
John P. M. Grier, Mount Jordan Pottery
Daniel High, Charlestown Pottery

Aaron James, Potter
Aaron James, Potter
Abraham James, Potter
Eber James
Jesse Kersey, Potter

Nathan Pusey Pottery
Joseph Roger Pottery
Benjamin Valentine Pottery
Carter Vickers Pottery
Thomas Vickers, Caln Pottery
John Vickers Pottery
Vickers Pottery at Lionville

More information on each pottery can be found in *The Potters and Potteries of Chester County, Pennsylvania* by Arthur E. James.

The following is a list of Chester county potters. The dates given indicate the time the potter was at the location stated.

Adams, John H.	Brandywine Township	1796-1802
Ash, Louis I.	Phoenixville	1901-03
Ashbaugh, John H.	Phoenixville	1902-03
Austin, Bertha E.	Phoenixville	1902-03
Austin, John	Phoenixville	1886-87

Austin, Robert	Phoenixville	1896-97
Austin, William	Phoenixville	1898-99
Bahling, Peter	Phoenixville	1890-91
Banks, William	Phoenixville	1850
Barton, Thomas	Phoenixville	1882-83
Bartzer, Frederick	Phoenixville	1902-03
Bartzer, Martin	Phoenixville	1896-97
Bayne, Taylor	West Chester	1842
Beech, John	Phoenixville	1890-91
Beerbower, R. W.	Phoenixville	c 1870
Bennett, Joshua	East Caln Township	1827-28
Binder, Henry	Brandywine Township	1801
Binnix, John	East Nottingham Township	1860
Binnix, John	Kennett Square	1870-75
Boyer, Nathaniel	Phoenixville	1896-97
Bradford, Samuel	East Nottingham Township	1850-52
Brosius, Daniel K.	Kennett Square	1847
Brosius, Edwin	Kennett Square	1847-85
Brosius, Mahlon	Londonderry Township	1820-28
Brosius, Mahlon	Upper Oxford Township	1828-63
Brown, Harvey	Phoenixville	1896-97
Brown, Herbert	Phoenixville	1902-03
Brown, Samuel	West Nottingham Township	1850
Brownback, Charles R.	Phoenixville	1898-99
Burns, John, Jr.	West Chester	1856-60
Burns, John, Jr.	Lionville	1865
Burns, Joseph P.	West Chester	1860
Butz, Milton	Kennett Square	1896-1903
Calhoun, Thomas	East Nottingham Township	c 1890
Carter, William	Londonderry Township	1808-12
Cavanauch, William A.	Kennett Square	1896-1903
Chalfant, Sherman	Phoenixville	1886-87
Chamberlain, John	Kennett Square	1860
Chamberlain, Thomas	East Nottingham Township	c 1860-90
Chantry, William	Phoenixville	1886-97
Chantry, William, Jr.	Phoenixville	1901-03
Coates, Levi	Londonderry Township	1806-60
Colgan, Rose	Phoenixville	1890-91
Cope, Caleb	Lincoln University	1893-1917
Cope, Darlington	West Chester	c 1831-40
Cope, Darlington	New London Township *	1840-52
Cope, Phillip D.	Lincoln University	1920-58
Cope, Wilmer	Franklin Township	1880-90
Cope, Wilmer	Lincoln University	1890-1943
Cowsson, Bowen	Westtown Township	1833
Cox, Bennett	Lionville	c 1845
Davis, Joel	Brandywine Township	1808-20
Dawson, Howard	East Nottingham Township	1865-80
Dean, Charles A.	Kennett Square	1902-05
Deilbert, Abbott L.	Phoenixville	1890-91
Devlin, William	Phoenixville	1882-91
Dietrich, David H.	Phoenixville	1898-99
Divinney, William	West Chester	1850
Donley, George P.	West Chester	1857-58

*Franklin Township, 1852-88

Donley, James P.**	West Chester	1850-63
Donley, John	Lionville	1886
Dougherty, James	Phoenixville	1886
Edwards,	Westtown	1842
Emery, L. Walter	Phoenixville	1896-97
Esbin, Isaac	London Grove Township	1847-49
Esbin, Isaac	Westtown Township	1850-55
Farrell, Joseph	Phoenixville	1896-97
Ferguson, William	Phoenixville	1902-03
Finland, Welford	Kennett Square	1896-97
Fisher, Thomas, Jr.	East Caln Township	1789-1802
Folk, Samuel	East Caln Township	1822
Foster, Philip	Phoenixville	1902-03
Ford, Jesse	Warwick Township	1749
Fraisure, Aaron	East Caln Township	1749-1802
Francis, Frederick	Warwick Township	1847-50
Fredericks, John	Lower Uwchlan Township	1858-60
Gamble, Benjamin	Kennett Square (kiln burner)	1896-1905
Garrison, James	Westtown Township	1860
Gilbert, Addison V.	Phoenixville	1882-83
Gilbert, Samuel	Phoenixville	1882-83
Gilbert, Samuel	Phoenixville	1882-83
Gilbert, William A.	Phoenixville	1882-83
Grier, E. Stanley	East Nottingham Township	c 1885-1915
Grier, James	East Nottingham Township	1828-56
Grier, James A.	East Nottingham Township	1870-71
Grier, James P. M.	East Nottingham Township	1835-66
Grier, Ralph J.	East Nottingham Township	1862-1902
Grier, Samuel H.	East Nottingham Township	c 1860
Grier, Thomas F.	East Nottingham Township	1884-89
Grier, Thomas L.	East Nottingham Township	1850
Hack, Alexander	Phoenixville	1882-83
Hack, Nicholas	Phoenixville	1867
Hall, John	West Whiteland Township	c 1816
Hamlin, George F.	East Nottingham Township	1871
Hartman, William, Jr.	Phoenixville	1896-97
Hendricks, John	Phoenixville	1858-60
Hickman, Emmor	Westtown Township	1801-07
High, Daniel	Charlestown Township	1808-25
Hoopes, Milton	Westtown Township	1833
Hoopes, Milton	Downingtown	1842-64
Hoopes, Milton	Lionville	1865-75
Hooker, Eri	East Nottingham Township	1880-90
Hooker, John	East Nottingham Township	1840
Howell, Nelson W.	Phoenixville	1886-1903
Howeraft, Thomas	Brandywine Township	1820
Huebner, George	Vincent Township	1796-1814
James, Aaron	Westtown Township	1728-53
James, Aaron	Westtown Township	c 1790-1823
James, Aaron, Jr.	Westtown Township	1820-21
James, Abraham	Westtown Township	1820-63
James, Eber	Westtown Township	1820-25
James, Eber	Downingtown	1825-28

**Also spelled Donnelly
c—circa

Kennedy, John	Phoenixville	1896-97
Kent, Daniel	Oxford	1870
Kersey, Jesse	East Caln Township	1794-1824
Kinsey, James	East Caln Township	1804
Klenk, Charles	Phoenixville	1902-03
Klenk, George	Phoenixville	1901
Klenk, William F.	Phoenixville	1898-99
Kurtz, Frank	Phoenixville	1896-97
Kustis, Paul P.	Phoenixville	1901
Ladd, Samuel	West Chester	1842
Latouch, William A.	Phoenixville	1886-87
Lawler, Patrick	East Nottingham Township	1865-69
Lawrence, Charles	East Caln Township	1822
Lewis, Jonathan	Westtown Township	1822, 1828-1829
Linker, John	Lionville	1850
Malone, Michael	Phoenixville	1898-99
Manion, John E.	Phoenixville	1902-03
Manion, Thomas	Phoenixville	1902-03
Manning, John	Phoenixville	1896-1901
Manning, Thomas	Phoenixville	1896-97
March, Edward	Phoenixville	1896-97
McCarraher	Phoenixville	1896-97
McMememin, William J.	Phoenixville	1890-91
Mendenhall, Jonathan	East Caln Township	1894-96
Michener, George C.	Phoenixville	1896-97
Miller, David	Phoenixville	1886-87
Minster, Evan	Westtown Township	1850-60
Mitchell, Joseph	Phoenixville	1886-87
Moore, Allen	Kennett Square	1850
Moore, Henry	Lionville	1842
Moore, Richard	Lionville	1857
Morrowson, John	New London Township	1850
Moyer, Charles E.	Phoenixville	1901-03
Mundall, James	East Nottingham Township	1860-71
Myers, Charles E.	Phoenixville	1890-91
Myers, Jacob	Phoenixville	1886-91
Notehelfer, John	Kennett Square	1860
Notehelfer, Michael	Kennett Square	1850-57
Pearson, John D.	Phoenixville	1882-83
Pearson, William	Phoenixville	1886-87
Phillips, Lewis	Phoenixville	1882-83
Pickel, Lewis	Kennett Square	1857
Pickel, Peter	Kennett Square	1857
Pusey, Nathan	East Caln Township	1796-1800
Pusey, Nathan	London Grove Township	1801-12
Reed, Isaac	Phoenixville	1898-99
Rees, Lemuel	Brandywine Township	1822-42
Reichling, John	Kennett Square	c 1918
Remmy, George	East Nottingham Township	c 1860
Remmy, Joseph B.	East Nottingham Township	1850
Rhodes, William W.	Phoenixville	1886-91
Ross, William E.	East Nottingham Township	1839-42
Royer, Albert	Phoenixville (pottery packer)	1898-99
Ruoss, George D.	Kennett Square	1901-02
Scheetz, Elmer E.	Phoenixville	1886-87

Schofield, Haines	Honey Brook	c 1888-95
Schofield, Henry, Sr.	East Nottingham Township	1854-69, 1873-85
Schofield, Henry, Sr.	Oxford	1869-72
Schofield, Henry, Jr.	Oxford	1869-72
Schofield, Henry, Jr.	East Nottingham Township	1872-80
Schofield, Henry, Jr.	Rock Springs, Md.	c 1900-44
Schofield, James W.	East Nottingham Township	1865-69
Schofield, James W.	Oxford	1869-72, 1890-91
Schofield, James W.	Reading, Pa. (for many years with Shenfelder's)	
Schofield, John	East Nottingham Township	1873-78
Schofield, John	Lionville	1879-84
Schofield, John	Oxford	1870-73, 1889-1905
Schofield, Stephen	Oxford	1869-73
Schofield, William	East Nottingham Township	1862-69, 1875
Schofield, William	Oxford	1869-72
Schofield, William	Lionville	1879-84
Schofield, William	Honey Brook	1888-1927
Schofield, William, Jr.	Honey Brook	c 1888-95
Seesholtz, George	Vincent Township	1796
Sharp, Frederick	Phoenixville	1886-87
Sherman, Samuel	Phoenixville	1902-03
Smedley, Enos	Westtown Township	1820-23
Smedley, Enos	Downingtown	1829-30
Smedley, Enos	West Chester	1831-54
Smith, George	Phoenixville*	1896-97
Smith, Henry	West Nottingham Township	1836-57
Spangel, Ludwig	East Whiteland Township	1768
Stretch, Samuel C.	East Nottingham Township	1871-73
Stretch, Samuel or Bill	Kennett Square	c 1880
Strong, Constantine	Kennett Square	1870-85
Taylor, George	Westtown Township	1850
Taylor, Washington	East Nottingham Township	1850
Terry, David	Phoenixville	1896-97
Trunk, Frederick	Phoenixville	1890-93
Trunk, Herman	Phoenixville	1898-99
Trunk, Jacob	Phoenixville	1886-1901
Trunk, William	Phoenixville	1886-87
Valentine, Benjamin	Westtown Township	1807-15
Valentine, Benjamin	East Caln Township (Coatesville)	1819-38
Vickers, John	East Caln Township	1796-1814
Vickers, John	West Whiteland Township	1814-22
Vickers, John	Lionville	1823-60
Vickers, John Lewis	Lionville	1868-73
Vickers, Joseph	West Chester	1860-63
Vickers, Isaac	East Caln Township	1822
Vickers, Paxson	Lionville	1835-66
Vickers, Thomas	East Caln Township	c 1796-1822
Vickers, Thomas	Lionville	1823-28
Vickers, Ziba	East Caln Township	1808-12
Vickers, Ziba	Londonderry Township	1812-14
Vickers, Ziba	Lionville	1842-48
Wagg, Thomas	Phoenixville	1890-91
Webb, Jacob	Westtown Township	1796

*member of the Phoenixville firm Griffen, Smith and Hill

Webber, Francis	West Chester	1842
Weir, Augustus	West Chester	1850
Wiseburg, Jacob	East Nantmeal Township	1782
Wood, Mahlon	Kennett Square	1857-70
Worrell, J. Percy	Kennett Square (pottery decorater)	1902-20
Yarnall, Charles J.	Phoenixville	1896-97
Yearsley, John	Westtown Township	1802-09
Yother, Jacob	East Caln Township	1796
Young, Elmber E.	Phoenixville	1896-97

The following forms of pottery are known to have been made in the county.

Aquariums
    Pedestal Stump

Banks
    Money

Basins
    Glazed

Baskets
    Hanging

Bowls
    Sugar
    Wash

Boxes
    Porch
    Window

Cakies

Candlesticks

Cans
    Fruit

Cellars
    Salt

Chambers
    With Lids

Churns

Colanders

Collars
    Stove Pipe

Coolers
    Water

Covers
    Pan
    Pot

Crocks
    Apple butter
    Sauer kraut

Cups
    Cream
    Flat
    Jelly
    Salt

Cylinders
    Long for stove pipes
    Short for stove pipes

Dishes
    Fern
    Pie
    Sauce
    Turk's Head

Footwarmers

Fountains
    Chicken

Guards
    Long pipe
    Short pipe

Jars
    Fruit with corks

Jugs
    Molasses
    Money
    Vinegar
    Water

Kegs
    Water

Logs
    Camp fire
    Gas

Molds
    Cake
    Jelly

Mugs
    Chamber
    Shaving

Pans
    Bed
    Bread
    Butter with covers
    Fern
    Kneading
    Milk
    Pudding

Pipkins

Pitchers

Plates
    Pie

Porringers

Pots
    Bean
    Butter
    Chamber
    Cheese
    Coffee
    Cream
    Flat
    Flower
        Aquarium
        Common
        Fancy
    Gardener's
    Green house
    Handled
    High
    Milk

Stew	Stands	Toys
Sugar	Fish glove	Animal
Tea	Ink	Assorted
Shakers	Umbrella	Vases
Sand	Stove pipe guards	Garden
	Stove supports	Yard
Spittoons	Tiles	Urns
Mantel	Drain	Flower
Shell	Roofing	Water coolers
	Water pipes	

Candlestick. Height 9 1/4".
Chester County Historical Society collection.

left   Jug marked "J KERSEY". He was apprenticed to John Thomson in Philadelphia. Later he became a potter, preacher, and promoter working in Brandywine and East Caln Townships, between ca. 1794 and 1829. Height 14″.
Chester County Historical Society collection.

right   Two gallon crock signed on the bottom "AARON JAMES 1805". He worked in Westtown Township, ca. 1790-1823. Height 12″, diameter 8″, diameter at top 4 1/2″.
Anonymous.

below   Turks Head height 4″, diameter 10″. Bean pot marked "Hannah Taylor September 10th 1818", height 10 1/2″. Bed Pan, 11 1/2″ by 9 1/2″.
Chester County Historical Society collection.

Signature on bottom of two gallon crock.

Birds. Left to right: height 5″, height 5 1/2″, height 3 1/2″.
Mrs. Herbert F. Schiffer collection.

left   Bank marked "Hannah Hibbert, August 28 1830". Height 6″.
        Mrs. Herbert F. Schiffer collection.

right   Flower pot marked "Mary Marshall Westtown Chester County 8th
        Mo 1820". Height 8″.
        Mrs. Herbert F. Schiffer collection.

below   Funnel, height 4″. Stove support, height 5″. Gigging light used for
        night fishing, height 5 1/2″, depth 17″. Shaving mug, height 3″, width
        3″, depth 3 1/2″.
        Chester County Historical Society collection.

Flower pot with scrafito decoration marked "Sarah Sheeleigh 1838 Uwchland Pottery." John Vickers learned the trade from his father Thomas Vickers at the Caln pottery which was in operation between 1796 and 1823. In 1814 John Vickers left his father and moved to West Whiteland Township. In 1823 he moved to Lionville, Uwchland Township. Both father and son typified the Chester County trilogy of being Quakers, potters and abolitionists. Height 8 1/2".

Mrs. Herbert F. Schiffer collection

Flower pot marked "John Vickers & Son, Lionville, Chester County, Pa." On the side is inscribed "Is this a Christian world?/ Are we a human race?/ And can man from his brother's soul/ God's imprint dare efface?" Height 8 1/2".
Chester County Historical Society collection.

Dish marked "C. M. Pugh December 25, 1841." Diameter 17".
Mr. and Mrs. Samuel W. Morris collection.

Toy made at the Hoopes Pottery, Downingtown between 1842 and 1864. Height 10 1/2".
Chester County Historical Society collection.

Bird cage marked "A V". Height 9″, width 7 1/2″, length 10 1/2″.
Chester County Historical Society collection.

Toys. The two large dogs are attributed to the Vickers Pottery. On October 18, 1832 Jacob Hause bought a Dozen toys at 90 cents per dozen from John V. Vickers. Height left to right: 5 1/2″, 2 1/2″, 5″.
Mrs. Herbert F. Schiffer collection.

Rockingham tea pot and pitcher made at the Mount Jordan Pottery in East Nottingham Township. The pottery was operated by members of the Grier family. "Rebecca at Well" tea pots were copied from those made in Bennington, Vermont. Teapot height 8 1/2", creamer height 6".

Chester County Historical Society collection.

Earthenware fireplace logs.

Chester County Historical Society collection.

Water filter, height 14 1/2" and chicken fountain height 15" made at the Mount Jordan Pottery in East Nottingham Township. They also made stoneware pots, jars, spittoons, milk pans, pitchers, fruit jars with corks, butter pans with covers, pot and pan covers and stone water coolers. The jug height 15" is inscribed "J. Kersey".
Chester County Historical Society collection.

Pitcher height 10", Crock height 6 3/4", Sander height 7" and Spittoon height 4".
Chester County Historical Society collection.

Porcelain made by John Vickers ca. 1824 in Lionville. The sugar bowl, height 5 1/2″ and the cream pitcher 5 1/2″ have "J V" on the bottom. The dessert plate, diameter 9″, is marked in red "John Vickers August 1824".

Chester County Historical Society collection

John Vickers mark.

Chester County Historical Society collection

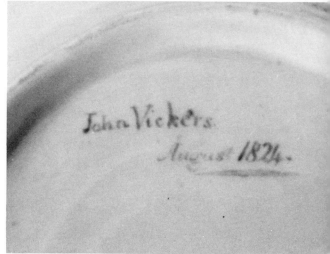

Majolica sugar bowl, height 5 1/2″; leaf dish 8 1/2″ by 7 1/2″; pitcher
5 3/4″.

Chester County Historical Society collection.

Majolica is the term applied to cream colored earthenware with
a lead or tin glaze, stained with coloring oxides to produce brilliant
effect. Majolica derives from a type of ware made in Majorca, Spain
from the fifteenth century. In France it was known as Faience and
in Holland as Delft.

In 1882 the first Etruscan majolica was made at the Phoenixville
Potteries, Starr and Church Streets, Phoenixville, Chester County. Between 1867 and 1882 the potteries had made yellow ware, Rockingham
ware, Parian, ornamental terra cotta and cream colored wares. In 1879
the pottery was leased to Henry Griffin, George Griffin, David Smith
and William Hill trading under the name of Griffin, Smith and Hill.
The designer was an Englishman named Bourne. It is the monogram
of this firm, the intertwining initials G S H, the initials and the words
Etruscan Majolica, the word Etruscan, or all three, which positively
identifies majolica ware made in Phoenixville.

Large quantities of Etruscan Majolica were purchased by the
Atlantic and Pacific Tea Company to be given away as premiums. Because of this there was a wide distribution of Phoenixville Majolica
in America. Many of the articles were ornamental objects with elabor-
ately modeled designs of animals, fish, vegetables and floral motifs
which had to be hand painted. Among the forms made were tea sets,
bowls, pitchers, spittoons and plates.

Majolica bowl. Height 8", depth 12".
Chester County Historical Society collection.

Walnut Cane Back Arm Chair attributed to John Knowles (d. Ridley Twp., 1778). Height 44", seat height 17½", width 18", depth 17½". *Chester County Historical Society collection.*

Beech Cane Back Side Chair attributed to John Knowles (d. Ridley Twp., 1778). Height 44", seat height 17½", width 18", depth 14¼". *Chester County Historical Society collection.*

Furniture

The following is a list of cabinet-makers, chair makers, clock-makers, joiners and turners working in the county prior to 1850. The dates given are working dates, unless preceeded by a "b" for birth, or a "d" for death. More information on these men can be found in *Furniture and Its Makers of Chester County, Pennsylvania* by Margaret Berwind Schiffer.

Acker (Acre), Henry 1798 d.1826
Acker, Jacob 1776 d.1823
Acker, Joseph D. 1850 d.1878
Aflick, Owen 1798
Ainsworth, John H. 1850
Aitkin, Abram 1850 d.1860
Aitken, John 1817 d.1839
Alcock, John 1828
Allen, Ephraim 1769-1773
Allen, Francis 1740
Allen (Alen), James d. 1811
Allen, John 1779
Allen, Josias 1765-1774
Allison, Aaron b. 1752-1802
Allison, Aaron R. 1850
Allison, Taylor 1841
Altemus, Marshall b.1819-1846
Amole, Edward 1798
Amole (Amold), Henry d.1848
Amole (Emol, Emold) 1804-1806
Anderson, Charles 1809
Anderson, David M. 1826 d.1862
Anderson, George W. 1847
Anderson, James 1790-1804
Anderson, Jesse 1821 d.1842
Andrew Jacob 1807
Andrews, Hugh 1828
Angus (Anguish), Jacob 1798-1801
Ankrim, Samuel 1799-1801
Armitt, Isaac, Jr., 1816
Armitt, Richard b. 1739 d.1790
Ash, Samuel b.1748-1782
Askew, Lazarus d.1771
Askew (Askue), William 1766-1767
Askin, Michael 1742-1754
Atherton, Benjamin 1829-1833
Atherton, Caleb 1788
Atherton, John d.1838
Ayars, Shepherd 1818 d.1856

Bags, James 1808
Baily, Charles 1807-1818
Baily, Emmor b.1767-1806
Baily, Israel b.1787-1804
Baily, Joel b.1732 d.1797
Baily, Levi b.1750 d.1809
Baily, Pennock b.1803-1829
Baily, Richard Downing b.1818-1842
Baily William 1838
Baily, William, Jr. 1814
Baily, William, Jr. 1816-1836
Baily, Yarnall b.1799 d.1862
Baker, Elias 1795
Baker, Joshua b.1771 d.1829
Baker, Lewis 1842
Baldwin, George W. b.1777 d.1844
Baldwin, Harlan b.1786-1809
Baldwin, Harlan 1828-1850
Baldwin, Henry 1819
Baldwin, Jesse b.1829
Baldwin, John 1819-1836
Baldwin, Joseph 1828
Baldwin, Levi, Jr. b.1808-1835
Baldwin, Lewis 1842-1850
Baldwin, Marlin 1842
Baldwin, Robert b.1775 d.1829
Baldwin, Robert 1850
Baldwin, Thomas F. H. 1827-1850
Baldwin, William 1785
Baldwin, William 1850
Baldwin, William 1831-1843
Baldwin, William R. 1842-1844
Bandalt, Levi 1785-1790
Bane, Jesse b.1755-1786
Barker, Henry 1805-1806
Barnes, Henry 1696-1697
Barnet, Francis 1822
Barnet (Barnett), Nathan 1827
Barnet, Sampson 1814-1823

Barrett, Arthur b.1709 d.1743
Bartlett, Edward M. 1833-1839
Barton, James 1726
Bartnam, James b.1701 d.1771
Bateman, John 1817 d.1835
Battin (Battan), James 1790 d.1811
Battin, John 1748 d.1799
Battin, William 1797-1798
Baugh (Bough), John b.1774 d.1841
Beakes, Abraham d.1703
Beary, Christian 1797 d.1833
Beaver, Devault b. 1756 d. 1837
Bechtel, Martin d.1809
Bechtel, Samuel 1786 d.1814
Bechtel, Samuel d.1848
Bechtell, Jacob 1791
Beidler (Boydler), Jacob b.1778 d.1864
Bellerjeau, Samuel 1823-1827
Beltz, Jacob 1819-1842
Benner, Daniel 1832 d.1894
Benner, John d.1847
Bennett, Abraham P. 1834-1842
Bennett, Enoch 1799-1802
Bennett, Imla J. 1842 d.1864
Bennett, James 1835-1842
Bentley, Eli b.1752-1783
Berry (Burry), Daniel 1767 d.1799
Berry Edward 1842
Best, John 1814
Best, Thomas 1758
Bethell, William d.1707
Bezer, William 1764
Bibby, John 1836
Bilson, John 1850
Binder, George M. 1839 d.1861
Binder, Michael 1850
Bing, Joseph 1813
Bisbean (Bisbing), Peter 1816-1821
Black, Alexander 1832-1850
Blankerpealer, Peter 1850
Blatchford, Thomas 1850
Bloom, John 1850
Blunston, John, Jr. d.1716
Bodley, James 1790 d.1826
Boges, Ephem 1787
Bolding, William 1779
Bond, Benjamin 1796
Boon, Andrew 1775
Boon, William 1772
Booth, Joseph 1833-1835
Bowman, John W. 1850 d.1860
Boyd, Andrew 1801-1806
Boyd, John C. 1834-1848
Boyd, John 1832 d.1867
Boyer, William 1830

Boyland, John d.1772
Brady, Noah 1797
Breaman, David 1837
Breckwell, John 1831-1834
Breltz, Jacob 1815
Brenholts, Joseph 1834
Briggs, William d.1814
Britt, Robert 1801-1810
Brogan, Benjamin 1811
Brooke, Isaac d.1835
Brookes, John 1814
Brooks (Brookes), Edward 1795-1809
Brooks, William 1804
Broomhall, Jacob 1804-1808
Brower, John 1778
Brown, Benjamin 1796
Brown, Daniel 1850
Brown, David 1840 d.1849
Brown, Jacob b.1724-1797
Brown, John 1800 d.1814
Brown, John 1756 d.1780
Brown, John 1829
Brown, Moses 1808
Brown, Samuel 1828
Brown, William 1809
Brown, William, Jr. 1806 d.1826
Buckingham, James 1745 d.1793
Buckwalter, Henry 1850
Buckwalter, John d.1810
Buffington, Joseph 1748 d.1785
Buffington, Richard d. 1748
Bulla, William 1798
Buller, William 1834-1835
Bullock, Aaron b.1688-1734
Bunn, Benjamin 1797 d. 1835
Bunn, George 1807 d.1856
Burchall & Wickersham 1822-1824
Burke, Edmund 1835
Burns, Thomas S. 1842
Burres, James 1807
Butcher, Zachery d.1755
Butler, Abner b. 1776-1802
Butler, Benjamin 1805-1807
Butler, Elijah 1796-1833
Butler, Elisha 1805 d.1821
Butler, Henry W. 1833
Butler, James 1815-1816
Butler, John, Jr. 1796 d.1831
Butler John Felt 1849
Butler, Joshua 1810
Butler, Noble 1801-1806
Butler Samuel 1842
Butler, Swayne 1799-1821
Butler & Bartlett 1835
Buzzard, Frederick 1754

Cain, Moses 1789-1797
Cain, Robert 1797
Cain Robert b.1799 d.1846
Caldwell, John 1749 d.1772
Caldwell, John 1783-1792
Caley, Samuel 1740 d.1787
Callahan, Samuel b. 1784-1808
Calvert, Daniel 1756-1758
Calvert, John 1747 d.1784
Calvin (Colvin), Robert 1775-1778
Camm (Cann), Henry 1740 d.1758
Campbell, Benjamin 1775
Campbell, William, Jr. 1842-1850
Canan, James 1832-1838
Canby & Nielson 1819
Carffrey, David 1850
Cark, William 1842
Carleton, Thomas b.1732 d.1803
Carmount, John 1792
Carpenter, Charles F. 1846
Carrell, Joseph b.1792-1832
Cauffman, John M. b.1812 d.1857
Cave, Joseph 1821-1834
Chalfant, Chalkley 1849
Chalfant, Henry d.1800
Chalfant, James 1829 d.1857
Chalfant, Jesse 1814
Chambers, Benjamin 1782-1794
Chambers, William b.1764 d.1813
Chambers, William R. 1835-1850
Chandlee, Benjamin, Sr. b.1685-1741
Chandlee, Benjamin, Jr. b.1723 d.1791
Chapman, John 1734 d.1774
Charles, Andrew 1804
Cheers, James K. 1850
Chrisman, George d. 1835
Chrisman, John d.1832
Church, Alexander 1821
Clark, James 1798
Clark, Joseph 1807
Clark, William 1838 d.1886
Claypoole, George 1760
Clingamen, Daniel 1842-1850
Cloud, James 1838
Cloud, William 1810 d.1826
Cloyd, John 1762 d.1782
Cloyd, Joseph C. 1849
Coates, Cromley 1850
Coates, Isaac b.1748 d.1809
Coates, Moses, Jr. 1773
Cochran, George 1801 d.1807
Colgin, William M. 1796
Colier, William 1848
Colin, Robert 1768 d.1781
Colt, Robert 1827-1828
Compton, John 1814

Compton, William 1814-1833
Conard Nicholas 1828
Connell, William 1768
Connerl, Samuel 1828
Conrad, Osborne 1835-1850
Cook, Samuel 1842
Cook, William 1748
Cookson, Thomas 1767
Cooper, Alpheus 1814-1821
Cooper, Calvin b.1766 d.1820
Cooper, Horatio G. b.1818 d.1900
Cooper, James b.1765 d.1817
Cope (Coope), Abiah 1811-1813
Cope, Ezra 1832-1833
Copeland, George 1804
Corfrey, David 1848
Corl, Abraham b.1779 d.1842
Crol, Conrad 1776-1790
Corl, Jacob 1802-1804
Corl, Mordecai 1842
Cornog, John 1830
Coston, B. P. 1829
Coulson, John 1772
Coulson, Thomas 1740 d.1763
Cowden, Franklin 1850
Cowders, James F. 1849
Craig, John 1821 d.1871
Creps, Michael 1809
Creton, Hugh 1747
Crewe, Samuel 1835-1850
Criswell, Charles 1816
Criswell, Elijah 1850
Cromberger, Charles 1842
Crosby, David 1781 d.1834
Cross, Henry 1835
Crow, Thomas 1850
Crow, Thomas 1808 d.1824
Crow, William 1850
Croyl, John 1797
Cryder, Adam 1773
Culbertson, Benjamin b.1751-1773
Culbertson, James 1800 d.1850
Cundy, William 1850
Cunsendouser, Richard d.1794
Custer (Custerd), Jesse 1796-1798
Cutler, Benjamin b.1740 d.1794

Dampman, John 1833-1835
Darlington, Abraham b.1723 d. 1799
Darlington, Amos b.1764 d.1828
Darlington, Amos, Jr. b.1792 d.1853
Darlington, Benedict b.1786 d.1864
Darlington, Brinton b.1781 d.1860
Darlington, Caleb b.1805 d.1890
Darlington, Samuel S. b.1795 d.1859
Darlington, Thomas b.1725 d.1808

Davidson, Francis b.1767 d.1848
Davies, Hugh d.1721
Davis, Amos 1745-1754
Davis, Caleb 1807-1808
Davis, David 1754 d.1788
Davis, John d.1720
Davis, John d.1848
Davis, Mary 1799
Davis, S. W. 1850
Davis, Samuel 1850
Davis, Shanon 1815
Davis, William d.1822
Davis, William 1835
Davis, William 1850
Davis, William R. 1831
Davison, Thomas 1844
Denny, Samuel 1820-1842
Derlin, John 1802
Derr, Andrew 1799
Derrick, Thomas 1759-1768
Dickey, John 1790-1810
Dickey, Samuel 1775-1794
Dickey, William 1799
Dickinson, Gaius 1814 d.1848
Diffendaffer, Henry d. 1848
Dillon, Josiah 1768
Dilworth, Joseph 1802
Dilworth Joseph 1789-1821
Dilworth, Richard d.1769
Dilworth, Thomas 1805
Dingee, Jacob 1771 d.1795
Divin, James 1814
Dixon, James 1835-1841
Dollton, Joel 1838
Don, John 1737
Donaldson, William 1765-1768
Dorey, Joseph L. 1824
Dorlan, George 1782
Dorlan, Isaac 1807-1842
Dorlan, John 1801-1807
Dorlan, Nathan 1782 d.1817
Dorlan, Samuel 1805-1828
Doughty, Jacob F. 1846
Downing, William W. b.1791 d.1873
Drennen, James 1799-1801
Dring, Thomas 1786-1798
Dubre, Nathan 1821
Dubree, Henry 1842-1860
Dunbar, Alexander 1814 d.1851
Dunbar, Mathew 1814
Dunkin, Aaron d.1792
Durnald (Dunnall), Thomas 1715-1718
Dutton, John 1739-1741
Dyer, Andrew 1835

Eachus, Daniel 1728 d.1805
Eachus, Robert 1763
Eachus, Virgil 1783 d.1839
Earley, Milton 1830
Eavenson, Benjamin 1833-1835
Eavenson, Joseph b.1795-1850
Eavenson, Ralph 1715 d.1744
Echoff (Eckhoff, Ecoff, Eachoff),
    David 1806 d.1848
Echoff, John 1842
Echoff, Samuel 1808
Edwards, John 1849
Edwards, Samuel d.1844
Eldridge, Jonathan d.1775
Elliott, Francis
Ellis, Elisha 1785-1790
Elton, Robert 1773-1794
Emery, Jacob d.1876
Emery, Ludwick 1786
Engers, Abraham d.1761
England, David b.1737-1773
England, Isaac b.1786 d.1860
Entrikin, James 1850 d.1863
Entrikin, Joseph 1823-1824
Entrikin, Philip W. 1840
Entrikin, Samuel 1837
Epright, Jacob 1850
Erwin, Ezekial 1785-1788
Esbin, Jesse 1824 d.1873
Evans, Elijah 1785
Evans, John 1778-1810
Evans, Joseph 1819-1821
Evans, Joshua 1760-1802
Evans, Lewis d.1733
Evans, Richard 1748-1762

Facundus, John 1796-1801
Farr, William 1737
Farran, James, Jr. d.1842
Faucett, James 1810
Fawkes, Samuel 1803-1808
Fell, Edward 1777-1790
Fell, Mark b. 1779 d.1840
Feree, William 1848-1850
Ferrel, Andres 1806-1835
Fertig, Jacob b.1788 d.1823
Few, William 1801
Filson, Francis 1842
Finger, Daniel 1808-1814
Finger, Daniel 1828-1850
Finger, Israel 1842 d.1895
Fisher, Jacob 1850
Fitzsimmons, George b.1780 d.1830
Fleming, Henry 1859 d.1865

Fletcher, Richard 1715-1721
Ford, Benjamin 1823
Ford, Thomas E. 1850 d.1862
Ford, Thomas Worth b.1806 d.1882
Ford, William 1788
Ford, William G. 1850
Fordham, Joseph 1755 d.1775
Foreman, Aaron W. 1835 d.1869
Foreman, Charles G. 1848 d.1886
Foreman, John b. 1762 d.1819
Foreman, John, Jr. b.1801 d.1879
Foreman, Jonathan 1826-1850
Foreman, Moses b.1806 d.1860
Foster (Fauster), John 1820-1832
Foulk, Daniel 1788-1791
Foy, Matthias T. 1811 d.1816
Francis, William d.1734
Frankum, John 1819-1821
Frazer, Joseph A. 1828
Fred, Benjamin 1738 d.1792
Fred, John 1779
Frederick, Benjamin 1805
Freed, George 1810 d.1843
Freeman, Henry B. 1847-1850
Frink, Jacob b.1717 d.1799
Funterwhite, John, Jr. 1832 d.1836
Fury, Robert Cory 1799-1805
Fussell, Bartholomew b.1754 d.1838
Fussell, William b.1728-1782

Gallagher, William 1832-1835
Gamble, Hamilton 1842-1850
Gambril, Robert 1828
Ganson, Francis 1801-1829
Garrett, Benjamin b.1771 d.1856
Garrett, Joseph b.1743 d.1792
Garrett, Joseph b.1773 d.1855
Garrett, Lewis 1808
Garver, Samuel 1850
Gatlive, Charles d.1743
Gault, William 1741-1823
Gawthrop, Allen b.1810 d.1885
Geroge, Matthew 1798-1827
Gest, Abraham 1789
Gibson, John d.1754
Gillespie, William d.1771
Gilpin, Thomas b.1700
Girtler, Jacob 1806
Girtler (Girtty), William 1840 d.1841
Girtley (Gertley), William 1809-1811
Glasby, Alban 1828
Glendening (Glendining), Adam
    1783 d.1812
Glendening, Adam 1825 d.1835

Goldsmith, Charles 1822-1823
Good, Francis, Jr. 1799 d.1857
Good, Robert 1832
Goodwin (Gooden), Elisha 1785-1797
Goodwin, Isaac 1783-1785
Goodwin, Richard 1762 d.1816
Goodwin, Thomas 1801 d.1840
Gottier, Francis 1786
Gougler, Philip 1802 d.1840
Gray, Thomas 1814-1829
Green, John 1805
Greenfield, John 1835-1838
Gregg, George 1796 d.1833
Gregg, Herman 1800
Gregg, Thomas 1821-1840
Griffith, Abijah 1785
Griffith, Abraham 1798-1805
Griffith, Ebenezer b.1792 d.1824
Griffith, James 1814 d.1855
Griffith, John 1834
Griffith, John C. 1850
Griffith, Joseph 1802
Griffith, Lewis 1824
Grubb, Isaac d.1839
Grubb, John d.1708
Guest, Mr. 1781

Haddock, John 1692
Hadley, John b.1782-1827
Haigana, William James 1830
Haines, David b.1773 d.1854
Haines, Edward 1802-1806
Haines, Jacob d.1811
Haines, John 1729-1741
Haines, John 1802
Haines, Rudolph 1783-1790
Hall, Charles 1759-1789
Hall, Elias 1821
Hall, Issac d.1848
Hall, John b.1691 d.1760
Hall, John b.1793 d.1867
Hall, Joseph 1838 d.1887
Hall, Reubin 1786-1775
Hamer (Harner, Hammer), Abel, Jr.
    1799-1809
Hamer (Harner, Hammer), Israel
    1799-1813
Hames, Edward 1805
Hammon (Hamon), Nobel 1807-1811
Hammer, John 1791
Hance, Joseph d.1830
Hand, James 1842
Hankel, Jacob d.1789
Hannum, James 1763 d.1823

Hans, Aaron 1800
Hanson, Hance 1809
Happer, Daniel 1823
Harbey, Robert 1739-1758
Harley, Rudolph S. 1842
Harner, Abraham 1795 d.1802
Harner, Israel 1799-1803
Harper, Ralph, Jr. 1741
Harris, George d.1752
Harris, John 1833
Harrison, Caleb 1779 d.1793
Harry, George 1792
Harry, Nathan 1850
Harshberger (Hershberger), John
   1810-1829
Hartman, John 1790
Hartman, John E. 1799 d.1842
Hartman, Moses 1814-1816
Harvey, Ellis 1824
Hatch, Jonathan 1814
Hassing (Hasson), John 1808-1811
Haverlin (Haverly) Christian 1759-1764
Hawley, Isaac b.1775 d.1836
Hawley, Thomas P. b. 1818 d. 1885
Hayes, Caleb 1808
Hayes, John d.1788
Hayes, Jonathan, 1755
Hayes, William 1799
Hayworth, John 1819-1823
Hayworth (Haworth), Warner 1814-1829
Heacock, John 1740 d.1794
Heacock, Nathan 1772 d.1825
Heaknass, George 1746
Hell, Jacob 1776
Henderson, Henry 1802
Henderson, James 1793 d.1813
Henderson, Joseph 1829
Henry, Samuel 1772 d.1773
Henry, William 1823-1826
Heslip, Thomas 1800-1801
Heston, Paul 1791
Hewes, Samuel 1756
Hibberd, Benjamin b.1707 d.1785
Hibbard, Caleb b.1781 d.1835
Hibbard, Joseph b.1700 d.1737
Hibberd, Moses b.1702 d.1762
Hick, Jonas d.1788
Hiestand, David d.1847
Hiestand, John b.1785 d.1880
Higgins, Benjamin 1850
Higgins, Franklin 1850
Higgins, James 1828-1850
High, Daniel d.1775
Hillis, William b.1752 d.1816
Himes, David 1835
Himmelwright, Philip 1788-1790

Hodges, Thomas 1719
Hoffman, George 1842 d.1845
Hoffman, Isaac 1804-1811
Hoffman, Philip 1816-1842
Hoffman, William 1846 d.1877
Holby, William 1836
Hollingsworth, Valentine 1789 d.1826
Hollis, George 1821-1822
Hollis, Joseph M. 1819-1821
Hollis, Thomas 1800
Holman, Conrad 1790-1802
Holser, Jacob 1821
Holstein, John Jones b.1785 d.1818
Hong, Aaron 1801 d.1807
Hoopes, Abraham b.1775 d.1823
Hoopes, Abram 1845-1850
Hoopes, Caleb, 1800-1807
Hoopes, Henry 1814
Hoopes, John b.1745 d.1831
Hoopes, Joseph b.1773 d.1830
Hoopes, Levi I. b.1813 d.1903
Hoopes, Levis b.1818-1842
Hoopes, Phineas b.1811 d.1865
Hoopes, Rees b.1782 d.1838
Hoopes, Simeon b.1816 d.1897
Hope, Robert 1796-1799
Hope, Tobias 1796
Horn, David 1810
Hosman, Lewis 1842
House, Amos b.1742 d.1821
House, Francis 1805-1806
House, James 1811-1844
House, Joseph 1835
House Nicholas 1799 d.1845
House Samuel 1771-1811
Howell, David 1762
Howell, Isaac 1758 d.1759
Howell, John 1844-1845
Howell, John M. b.1818 d.1876
Howel, Samuel 1808
Howell, Thomas d.1802
Howell, Thomas 1801-1807
Hughes, Ellis b.1792 d.1840
Hughes, Grover d.1833
Hughes, Samuel 1768
Humphrey, Rebecca 1785-1799
Humphrey, Robert 1819
Humphreys, Joshua b.1743 d.1810
Humphrys, Samuel 1752-1760
Hunt, Joseph b.1781-1808
Hunt, Roger 1740 d.1764
Hunt, William 1850
Hunter, Henry 1754
Hunter, Joseph 1842
Huss, Jacob 1808-1809
Huss, Nicholas 1809

Hutchinson, James 1850
Hutchinson, Thomas 1808-1816
Hutton, Benjamin b.1728 d.1797
Hutton, Hiet b.1756 d.1833
Hutton, Jesse b.1752 d.1811
Hutton, Thomas b.1758-1801
Hyatt, William 1850

Ingram, John J. 1843
Irwin, Alexander 1798 d.1814
Irwin, William 1835-1850

Jackson, Caleb b.1821 d.1856
Jackson, Cyrus 1842
Jackson, George 1799 d.1836
Jackson, Isaac b.1734 d.1807
Jackson, Isaac, Jr. b.1746 d.1795
Jackson, John 1800 d.1822
Jackson, Jonathan d.1793
Jackson, Joseph H. 1835 d.1857
Jackson, Samuel 1795
Jacobs, James 1742
Jacobs, Samuel 1831-1850
James, Enoch 1762-1763
James, James 1762
James, Jonathan 1816
James, Jonathan, Jr. 1804-1816
Jefferis, Bennett 1839
Jefferis, Emmor 1830
Jefferis, James 1830-1834
Jefferis, Nathaniel b.1733 d.1823
Jefferis, Thomas 1774-1783
Jefferis, William 1697 d.1778
Jefferis, William, Jr. b.1729 d.1777
Jenkins, George W. 1834
Jenkins, J. 1834
Jenkins, Thomas 1792-1803
Job, Daniel 1838
John, Amos 1779 d.1832
John, Amos P. 1850
John, Eneas P. 1849 d.1862
John, Obia 1822
John, Reuben 1769-1813
John, Robert 1796-1799
John, Samuel 1749-1766
John, Thomas d.1731
Johns, William 1813-1814
Johnson, David 1842
Johnson, Joseph 1835
Johnson, George R. 1850
Johnston, John 1819
Johnston, Joshua 1850
Johnston, Thomas 1781-1785
Johnston, William 1767-1787
Jones, Benjamin 1790 d.1815
Jones, Enoch d.1833

Jones, Griffith d.1805
Jones, John d.1755
Jones, Jon 1825
Jones, John 1758-1799
Jones, Joseph 1817 d.1868
Jones, Lewis 1806-1807
Jones, Richard 1718-1727
Jones, Samuel 1810 d.1826
Jones, Thomas d.1766
Jones, William 1818
Jordon, Stewart 1796-1797
Josinskey, Frederick 1814
Joyce, Richard 1846-1847

Keeler, Owen d.1741
Keemer, James 1828
Keemer, John 1828
Kehn, Samuel 1828
Kelsby, Joseph d.1747
Kelton, John 1731
Kenny, Thomas 1804
Kerchner, Peter 1842
Kerns, Miller 1842-1846
Kerr, William 1850
Kersey, Samuel 1831 d.1840
Kester, Paul 1789-1791
Keylor, John 1850
Kichen, Enoch 1809
Kiemer, John 1812 d.1867
Kimble, John 1793-1815
Kimes, Henry 1782
Kinkead, James 1765
Kinsey, George 1789-1796
Kirk, Caleb 1760-1768
Kirk, Elisha b.1757 d.1790
Kirk, Joseph 1783
Kirk, William b.1719 d.1767
Kirk, William 1850
Kirkpatrick, Francis 1800-1801
Knauer, Christopher d.1811
Knauer, Christopher d.1832
Knauer, David 1840 d.1857
Knauer, John 1818
Knowles, John d.1778
Knox, Timothy 1772
Kuller (Kuler, Kohder), George W.
    1846-1850
Kurtz, Joseph d.1815

Laar, Geroge 1814
Lackey, James 1800-1822
Lahr, John d.1843
Lamborn, Jacob Kirk b.1816-1841
Lammy, Edward 1811 d.1813
Lamphear, Elihu D. 1829
Landis, Jacob 1791-1795

Landis, Solomon 1809
Lapp, David d.1824
Larkin, William d.1763
Lashey, Thomas 1764
Lattimone, George 1748-1750
Lauer & Brown 1813
Lawkin, Stephen H. 1850
Lawrence, John 1788 d.1842
Lawrence, Mondecai 1785-1799
Lawrence, Samuel 1788 d.1814
Lea, Armot W. 1850
Lee, Caleb 1850
Lee (Lea), Nathan 1824
Leed, Norman 1803
Lefever, Daniel 1816
Lefever, John 1799-1801
Lefever Sameul 1805 d.1848
Letchworth, John 1823-1824
Levis, Samuel b.1680 d.1758
Lewis, Abel 1801 d.1835
Lewis, Griffith d.1737
Lewis, Jefferson 1825-1829
Lewis, Joseph 1835-1850
Lewis, Nathan 1805-1806
Lewis, Nathan H. 1827
Lewis, Richard 1727
Lewis, William 1707
Lewis, William d.1777
Lichtanthaler, Benjamin 1842-1843
Lightfoot, John d.1835
Lightfoot, Thomas d.1725
Lillis, Edward 1805
Lilly, David 1783
Lincoln, Mordecai b.1802-1850
Lincoln, William b.1780-1850
Littler, Samuel d.1727
Littleton, Thomas 1824
Llewellyn, John 1762
Llewellyn, William 1806 d.1825
Lloyd, Thomas R. 1850
Logan, Eli 1814
Logan, Henry 1798-1815
Logan, William d.1841
Long, Albert 1850
Long, Joseph 1840-1850
Long, Robert W. 1850
Longacre, John 1800 d.1844
Longstreth, Benjamin b.1746 d.1802
Lowry, Samuel 1715
Ludwick, John 1850
Lumerit, Thomas 1850
Lutts, Henry 1809-1810
Lyon, William 1754-1763

McClean, Henry 1807
McClean (McClain), William 1850

McCleary, Thomas 1767
McClellan, John b.1766-1814
McClellan, Mary 1814
McClellan, Samuel 1779 d.1808
McClellan, Samuel P. 1813-1818
McCluchen, Henry 1842
McColgin, William 1796-1841
McConaghy, William 1829 d.1858
McConnell, J. Clemens no date
McCordick (McCordic), William
    1800-1828
McCook, John 1748-1754
McCoskey, James 1757-1762
McCullough, John 1818 d.1834
McCullough, Thomas, Jr. 1812
McDurman, Lewis 1842-1844
McFarlan, George b.1772-1815
McFarlan, Samuel 1796-1807
McFarlan, William d.1782
McFarlin, William 1804
McGoughlin, William 1765-1771
McGugin, James 1814 d.1819
McGugin, Jesse 1850
McGuigan, Patrick 1827
McGuigan, Patrick, Jr. 1814-1835
McIntire, Alexander 1844
McIntire, Andrew 1773-1775
McIntire, Samuel 1817-1823
McKinsey, Kenneth 1799
McLoad, Norman 1799-1801
McMinn, James 1799 d.1828
McMinn, John 1802 d.1850
McMinn, Joshua 1799 d.1837
McNeal, James 1836
McNeil, James d.1841
McNutt, Ezra 1850
McTann, George 1835
McWilliams, George 1816
McWilliams, Robert 1835-1842
McWilliams, Samuel 1850
Maccy, Archibald 1754
Mace, Joseph 1796
Mackey, John 1850
Mackey, Robert 1804
Maddock (Madox), John 1689-1698
Major, William J. 1829-1842
Mallenbrock, Joseph 1842
Mansfield, John 1779
March, Frederick 1807 d.1835
March, Henry 1808
Marcum, Edward 1822
Marrock, William 1802
Marsh, Thomas B. 1835-1850
Marshal, Abajah 1842
Marshall, Humphrey 1805 d.1860
Marshall, J. 1840

Marshall, Jacob B. 1835-1850
Marshall, John 1772-1783
Marshall, Samuel 1842
Marshbark, John 1834-1837
Martin, George 1739 d.1780
Martin, Thomas 1770 d.1786
Mason, Benjamin 1835 d.1888
Mason, George 1828 d.1831
Mason, George 1828-1838
Matlack, George B. 1850
Matlack, Jonathan, Jr. 1811 d.1829
Matlack, Reuben 1828-1837
Matson, Eli 1826 d.1838
Matthews, Boaz d.1785
Maule, Joseph 1823-1825
Maxwell, Henry 1802
Mears, John 1737-1819
Mechem, John 1797-1802
Megilligan, John 1823 d.1875
Mendenhall, Caleb, Jr. b.1781 d.1856
Mendenhall, Caleb 1850
Mendenhall, Isaac b.1766-1790
Mendenhall, John 1715-1718
Mendenhall, Moses 1797-1818
Mendenhall, Samuel 1827-1830
Meredith, Isaiah 1849
Meredith, John 1837 d.1848
Meredith, Lewis B. 1850 d.1863
Michener, John 1799-1813
Michener (Mitchener), Rynear 1809
Michener, William S. d.1847
Mickle, John 1829
Miles, Edward 1756
Miles, Enos 1786 d.1806
Miles, John d.1776
Miles, William 1836
Millard, James 1800-1802
Miller, George 1850
Miller, Henry 1791 d.1859
Miller Joel 1776
Miller, John b.1665 d.1715
Miller, John 1826
Miller, Nicholas d.1787
Miller, Philip 1785 d.1803
Miller, Samuel 1792 d.1857
Miller, Stephen b.1794 d.1859
Miller, William 1842
Miller, William 1850
Milleson, Jonathan 1797
Millhouse, Asa 1829
Millhouse (Milhous), James b.1727-1773
Millhouse, John 1756-1771
Millhouse, Samuel 1783-1786
Millhouse, Thomas d.1873
Millington, Isaac 1842-1850
Mills, George 1828-1829

Mills, John d.1781
Mills, Robert 1732-1739
Milner, Nathan 1765-1767
Mitchel, Samuel 1827
Mitchell, Edward 1828-1846
Mitchem, John 1796
Mode (Moode), Alexander b.1713 d.1750
Moffet, Robert 1784-1787
Moon, Anselem 1801
Moon, Samuel 1803-1811
Moore, Anselon 1821
Moore, Charles 1842-1850
Moore, David b.1769 d.1823
Moore, David A. 1849-1850
Moore, Eli b.1769 d.1812
Moore, George, 1842-1850
Moore, George L. 1850 d.1880
Moore, Jacob b.1781-1814
Moore, Jeremiah b.1803 d.1887
Moore, Joshua b.1791-1814
Moore, Mordecai 1783-1795
Moore, Robert 1774-1820
Moore, Sharpless b.1809 d.1897
Moore, Thomas 1821
Moore, Thomas 1821
Moore, William 1798-1799
Moore, William 1828-1835
Moore, William 1842
Moore, William 1850
Moore, William C. 1835
Moore, Ziba b.1800-1835
More, Hanson 1821
Morgan, Thomas d.1763
Morgan, Thomas 1807
Morrel, John 1796
Morrill (Morrell), Robert 1764-1766
Morris, Chas. 1764-1766
Morris, Samuel 1795 d.1809
Morton, Taylor 1840 d.1861
Mullin, Joseph M. 1850
Murphy, John 1790
Murphy, Samuel 1850
Myers, Casper 1849

Nelson, William d.1831
Nichols, William 1731
Nicholson, Colberth 1741
Nields, Amos b.1805-1850
Nields, Daniel b.1810 d.1872
Nields (Neal, Neld), Elias 1745-1785
Nields, Joseph d.1839
Nielson, Alexander 1819-1821
Noblett, Dell b.1777-1810
Noblett (Noblit), Richard d.1764
Noblett (Noblit), William b.1700 d.1777
Norton, Samuel P. d.1826

Nutt, John 1790-1810
Nutt, William 1835-1841
Nyce, Phillip 1800 d.1821

Ogden, Benanuel b.1750 d.1836
Ogden, George b.1726 d.1762
Ogden, Thomas b.1790 d.1841
Oldham, Robert d.1749
Olwine, Abraham 1821-1824
Olwine, Henry 1812 d.1867
O'Neal (O'Neil), Francis 1799-1842
O'Neal, James 1821
Orin, Wilson b.1824 d.1852
Ottey (Otty), Eli b.1760 d.1857
Ottey (Otty), Enoch b.1814 d.1910
Ottey, James 1740 d.1766
Ottey, James 1755
Ottey (Otty), John 1835
Otty, Thomas 1842
Owen, John 1726 d.1752
Owens, William 1737-1758
Owen & Pyle 1781

Painter, Philip b.1777
Painter, Richard 1804-1808
Pancoast, Samuel 1773-1799
Pancoast (Penncost), Seth 1750 d.1792
Parker, Abraham 1741 d.1752
Parker, William 1807-1810
Parrot, William 1842
Pasker, James 1779
Paubert, George 1835
Paul, David 1798 d.1814
Peal, William 1803-1811
Pearce, Cromwell, Jr. 1812
Pearce, George 1684-1698
Pearce, John 1823-1850
Pearson, George b.1789-1823
Pearson, James 1814
Pearson, Nathan 1781-1799
Peirce, Hannah 1804-1810
Peirce, Joseph b.1761 d.1847
Pennell, Abram b.1753 d.1840
Pennell, Thomas b.1712 d.1750
Pennock, Joshua b.1757 d.1854
Pennock, Nathaniel b.1777 d.1849
Pennock, Samuel b. 1754 d. 1843
Pennypacker, Aaron 1842 d.1853
Pennypacker, Henry 1816 d.1846
Pennypacker (Pennepacker), Jesse d.1838
Pennypacker, Matthias d.1808
Peoples, Alexander d.1820
Perch, Conard 1804-1805
Perry, John 1730-1740
Pettit, Charles 1798

Petty, William 1790 d.1801
Philips, William d.1737
Phillips, James 1837
Phillips, Josiah, Jr. 1806
Phillips, Llewellin 1699-1704
Phipps, Crosby b.1769 d.1832
Phipps, Crosby b.1802 d.1841
Phipps, John P. b.1803 d.1840
Phipps, Jonathan 1804
Phoenix, John 1745-1755
Pickel, Adam 1850
Pierce, Thomas 1798-1810
Pim, Nathan 1805-1811
Pinkerton, Samuel 1799-1850
Planton, John 1835
Pleem, Christian 1804
Plowman, William 1790-1799
Pollock, Robert 1842
Pontzler, John 1816-1845
Porter, Robert 1775-1780
Powell, David b.1795 d.1829
Powell, William 1775-1785
Pratt, Daniel 1825
Preston, Joseph, Jr. b.1779 d.1834
Price, George 1818-1830
Price, John 1776-1786
Price, Susan H. 1850
Price, William 1842
Price, William H. 1822 d.1879
Priest, Isaac 1801-1812
Prizer, Daniel 1799-1800
Prizer, Frederick b.1764 d.1820
Pryer, Joseph 1770
Pugh (Pew), James 1775 d.1817
Pugh, Hugh d.1749
Pusey, Isaac b.1778 d.1842
Pyle, Eli 1802-1804
Pyle, Enoch 1828-1829
Pyle, Isaac 1841
Pyle, James d.1748
Pyle, John 1827-1828
Pyle, Joseph 1756 d.1811
Pyle, Levi b.1743 d. 1812
Pyle, Moses 1735 d.1821
Pyle, Stephen 1798

Quaintance, Joel 1835 d.1845
Quillian, Thomas 1739

Ramsey, James 1803
Ramsey, Robert 1800-1808
Ramsey, William 1835
Raphun, John 1815
Rapp, Frederick d.1833
Rea, Jacob B. 1850

Reed, Andrew 1842-1847
Reed, John 1842
Reese, Henry 1787 d.1826
Regensburg, Moses A. 1835-1842
Rehn, Samuel 1830
Reigner, Joseph 1842
Rejands, Thomas 1807
Rembaugh, George D. 1842-1850
Renshaw, James 1847 d.1857
Restine, John 1850
Retzer, Michael 1816-1817
Reynolds, Francis 1719-1760
Reynolds, Henry 1729
Reynolds, Henry 1850
Reynolds, John b.1695-1749
Reynolds, Samuel 1752-1769
Reynolds, William B. 1842-1850
Rhoads, John 1779
Rice, John 1798-1806
Richards, Jonathan 1790-1795
Richards, Joseph 1737 d.1756
Rigg, Clemment 1801-1820
Rigg, Robert 1782
Righter, Jacob 1790 d.1812
Riley, Richard 1754 d.1820
Rineard, John 1842
Rinehart, David d.1807
Rinehart, Peter 1776-1781
Rinewalt (Rhinewalt), David 1796 d.1816
Ring, Benjamin 1739 d.1767
Ring, Nathaniel 1767
Robinett, Allin d.1759
Robinett, Allin 1768
Roberts, David 1717-1722
Roberts, Israel 1788-1799
Roberts, James 1834-1835
Roberts, Leonard F. 1829
Robinson, John d.1816
Robinson, John V. 1839-1850
Rogers, Alexander 1798-1800
Rogers, Samuel d.1843
Rogers, Thomas 1850
Romans, Evan 1814-1817
Romans, John 1829
Ross, Alexander 1713-1714
Ross, Thomas 1829
Ross, William, Jr. 1807
Rowles, Hezekiah 1753-1771
Rudolph, Samuel 1823
Ruppert, Benjamin 1828
Russell, Hezekiah d.1831
Russell, James J. 1850
Russell, Obed 1810
Ruth, Francis 1767
Ruth, Henry d.1823

Ruth, James 1768
Rutherford, James 1769 d.1808

Samms, Nathaniel 1785
Samuals, Joseph d.1793
Sanderson, Samuel 1805-1807
Sands, John 1835
Saylor, Abner 1835
Scarlet, Shadrack 1757-1762
Scholfield, Nathan C. 1811-1814
Schreder, Magness 1764
Scott, John d.1716
Scott, John W. 1821-1829
Scott, Moses 1737-1758
Scott, Thomas b.1813-1846
Seal, Caleb 1821-1859
Seal, William 1800-1810
Seed, Eli 1828 d.1854
Sell, Jonathan 1719-1722
Serman, Thomas 1814
Shaner, George 1809-1810
Sharp, Eli 1800
Sharples, Abraham b.1748 d.1771
Sharples, Daniel b.1710 d.1775
Sharpless, Henry P. b.1813 d.1890
Sharpless, Jacob b.1741 d.1802
Sharpless William b.1752 d.1817
Shearer, Charles 1842
Shearman (Slearman, Sheerman,
    Spearman), Robert 1772-1805
Sheliday, Oliver 1841-1846
Shenemen, Joseph d.1875
Shimer, Frederick 1798
Shoemaker, Jonathan 1759
Shoemaker, William 1802-1813
Sidwell, Hugh 1754 d.1791
Sidwell, Nathan 1781-1810
Simecon, Isaac 1779
Singles, John 1842
Sleigh, Samuel 1796-1797
Sloyer, Henry d.1798
Smedley, Thomas b.1723 d.1811
Smedley, William b.1728 d.1766
Smith Heister 1850
Smith, Isaac 1791-1809
Smith, James d.1822
Smith, James 1842
Smith, James 1843-1847
Smith, James 1848
Smith, James 1850
Smith, James 1850
Smith, John 1779
Smith, John 1791
Smith, John 1798-1847
Smith, John 1850

Smith, Joseph B. no date
Smith, Mathew 1850
Smith, Robert 1802
Smith, Thomas 1771
Smith, Thomas M. 1842
Smith, Valentine, Jr. d.1811
Smith, William d.1780
Smith, William B. 1850
Snyder, Frederick 1806-1808
Snyder, John 1835 d.1847
Sower, Daniel 1844 d.1902
Speakman, Elisa 1786
Speakman, Hayes 1818 d.1870
Speakman, Joshua 1800 d.1850
Springer, Abraham 1831
Springer, Robert 1842 d.1853
Stanhope, Jacob 1834-1835
Stanley, Joseph 1850
Stanly, Joseph B. 1849
Stapleford, Thomas d.1720
Starr, Jeremiah d.1791
Starret, James 1821
Starrett (Starritt, Sterrett), James
   1786-1803
Steel, John 1850
Steele, William ca.1785
Steen, Isaiah 1796
Steinmetz, Daniel 1812-1842
Stephey, Philip 1786
Stern, Jacob 1801
Stewart, Charles 1830-1832
Stewart, John 1801-1802
Stigers, Joseph 1829
Stonemets, Daniel 1810-1842
Streater, Robert d.1718
Streby, William 1850 d.1873
Strode, Caleb d.1768
Stroud, James 1842
Strough, Mary 1788
Stuart, William d.1826
Sturges, Nathan 1788
Sudow, William 1821
Sugar, Samuel 1742
Sugar (Shugars), Thomas 1772 d.1789
Sugar, Thomas, Jr. b.1738 d.1820
Sumption, Isaac 1774-1785
Sutterfield, Samuel 1804
Swaggers (Swagor), Elisha 1800 d.1809
Swann, Moses 1739
Sweeten, John 1842-1845
Sweeten (Swaten), William 1830-1842
Sweney, Charles T. 1850
Sweney, William 1839-1850

Taggart, James 1835-1842
Taggart, John d.1792

Tanner, William 1850
Taylor, Ephraim 1818 d.1853
Taylor, Hiram 1835-1836
Taylor, Isaac 1812
Taylor, James 1814
Taylor, Job b.1770-1801
Taylor, Joel b.1786-1808
Taylor, John 1756-1812
Taylor, John 1850
Taylor, John F. 1842 d.1875
Taylor, Joseph 1699 d.1744
Taylor, Joseph d.1818
Taylor, Mordecai b.1713 d.1747
Taylor, Samuel 1806-1813
Taylor, Thomas 1816-1818
Teeny, Michael 1802
Temple, Milton D. 1835
Temple, Thomas d.1818
Terrett, Peter 1758
Thomas, Amos 1768
Thomas, David d.1734
Thomas, David d.1767
Thomas, David d.1824
Thomas, Eli b.1782-1811
Thomas, Enos b.1747 d.1805
Thomas, George W. b.1802-1842
Thomas, Hezael 1782-1805
Thomas, Isaac b.1721 d.1802
Thomas, Isaac 1767-1847
Thomas, Jonathan 1826
Thomas, Joseph 1796-1799
Thomas, Mordecai b.1767 d.1837
Thomas, Morris 1745-1758
Thomas, Nathan 1824
Thomas, Richard b.1672 d.1744
Thomas, Thomas b.1687 d.1774
Thomas, Townsend 1788-1789
Thomas, William 1782 d. 1798
Thomas, William 1843-1844
Thomas, William R. 1841
Thompson, Caleb P. 1840-1849
Thompson, John 1798-1801
Thompson, Robert 1799-1808
Thompson,William, Sr. b.1765-1828
Thompson, William, Jr. b. 1806 d. 1842
Timanus, Conrad Charles 1804
Titlow, Abraham 1837
Titlow, David d.1837
Todd, Samuel 1801
Townsend, John 1811
Townsend, Roger D. 1834
Trainer, Albert G. 1835
Tucker, John 1785 d.1810
Tucker, Thomas 1775-1782
Turner, William 1828-1849
Tyson, Isaac d.1846

Tyson, William 1768

Umstead, John 1832
Underwood, David 1793-1812
Underwood, George b.1814 d.1857
Urner, Martin, 1715 d.1755

Valentine, Benjamin d.1839
Valentine, John S. 1813
Valentine, Thomas 1842-1850
Valentine, Thomas S. 1810-1830
Van Nostan, Edward H. 1830-1831
Vasdine, Benjamin 1799-1805
Vesler, George 1782
Vibber, Russell no date
Vickers, Joshua b.1783 d.1807
Virtue, Robert 1822-1824

Wagner, Philip 1786
Walker, Benjamin d.1796
Walker, George 1804
Walker, Lewis d.1728
Walker, David 1799-1800
Walker, James 1762-1766
Wallace, Alexander 1734-1743
Wallace, Caleb 1849
Wallace, James 1802
Wallace, William 1752-1753
Walley, William d.1837
Walter, William 1799-1801
Waltmire, John 1849
Walton, Elish (Lisha) 1842-1846
Walton, Jerome b. 1835 d.1876
Warner, John 1807-1814
Warren, Amos 1797-1809
Warren, James 1796-1803
Warren, John 1796
Wartnaby, Edward d.1715
Waterman, Charles 1821-1823
Waterman, Hannah 1832
Waterman, Phineas 1830-1844
Watkin, Robert 1807
Watt, Samuel 1850
Way, Chandler 1850
Way, David 1850
Way, David M. b.1818 d.1895
Way, Jacob b.1797 d.1848
Way, Jesse 1850
Way, John b.1772 d.1848
Way, John b.1766-1796
Way, John 1802-1803
Way, Joseph 1734
Way, Moses b.1801 d.1880
Way, Paschall 1849-1850

Wayne, Humphrey 1744-1752
Weaver, Isaac 1806 d.1863
Weaver, Jeremiah 1828
Webb, Benjamin 1764 d.1765
Webb, Daniel d.1773
Webb, James 1808-1809
Webb, John B. 1822
Welch (Welsh), Elisha 1817 d.1846
Welsh, George W. 1850
Wentz, John T. d.1848
Werster, George b.1751 d.1832
Westler (Wetsler), Casper 1805 d.1816
Whitaker, Reuben 1802-1806
White, Andrew 1850
White, Benjamin 1799-1800
White, Ezekiel 1809 d.1860
White, John 1828-1840
White & Pearson 1814
Whitehead, William 1829
Whiteside, Nathan 1850
Whittsitt, George 1734 d.1736
Wickersham, Amos b.1773-1814
Wickersham, Enoch b.1739 d.1836
Wickersham, Gideon b.1773 d.1848
Wickersham, Isaac b.1784 d.1857
Wickersham, James b.1712 d.1804
Wickersham, Levi b.1784 d.1865
Wickersham, Peter b.1792 d.1854
Wickersham, Thomas 1735
Wickersham, William 1842
Wilde (Wielde), Isaac T. 1848 d.1857
Wiley, Alexander 1810
Wiley, Caleb 1814-1815
Wiley, James S. 1850
Wiley, John 1818
Wiley, William H. 1823
Wilkey, George 1802
Wilkinson, Francis 1775 d. 1852
Wilkinson, Josiah S. 1842
Wilkinson (Wilkenson), Lee 1837
Wilkinson, Samuel 1799
Wilkinson, Thomas b.1745 d.1813
William, William 1842-1858
Williams, Benjamin 1827
Williams, David 1796
Williams, Edward d.1748
Williams, Issachar 1797
Williams, James 1813
Williams, Jesse 1774
Williams, John 1835
Williams, Josiah 1840
Williams, Moses 1821
Williams, Thomas 1739
Williams, William 1829-1835
Williams, William 1850

Williams, William d.1834
Williamson, Charles 1816
Williamson, James d.1848
Williamson, Robert Barclay 1846
Williamson, William 1838
Willis, William 1795
Wilson (Willson), Benjamin 1764-1811
Wilson, David b.1805 d.1864
Wilson, James 1804
Wilson, John 1744-1746
Wilson, John 1807-1832
Wilson, Joseph 1735-1758
Wilson, Joseph 1805
Wilson, Robert 1790-1839
Wilson (Willson), Samuel 1766 d.1790
Wilson, Samuel 1808-1809
Wilson, Silas 1830
Wilson, Smith 1850
Wilson, Smith T. 1850
Wilson, Thomas 1714
Wilson, Thomas 1741 d.1826
Wilson, William 1835
Windle, Jonathan b.1779 d.1862
Windle, Moses, b.1754 d.1788
Windle, William b.1739 d.1825
Withrow, Andrew 1814
Withrow, John 1833-1846
Witman, John d.1823

Wolf, Thomas D. 1814 1815
Wollaston, John d.1839
Wood, Joseph 1805-1850
Woodside, Archibald 1800
Woodward, David B. 1842 d.1888
Woodward, Jacob 1817-1822
Woodward, John b.1749 d.1808
Woodward, Maris D. b.1814 d.1892
Woodward, Miller b.1811 d.1879
Woodward, Thomas b.1753 d.1837
Worley, Nathan 1736
Worrall, Peter d.1767
Worth, John b.1745 d.1790
Worth, Joseph b.1782 d.1868

Yarnall, Allen b.1803 d.1832
Yarnall, Samuel b.1710 d.1749
Yearsley, James 1828
Yocum, Jacob 1850
Young, George 1837
Young, James b.1783 d.1814
Youngblood, Henry 1804
Yule, Thomas d.1783

Zell, David 1850
Zigler, Christopher d.1792
Zubin, David 1799 d.1803
Zubin, John d.1847

INLAID FURNITURE

Line inlay, the most common superimposed decorative device for furniture is also known in Chester County. In most of the pieces located, the inlay in the category consists of initials and dates.

Turning, scalloping, and the use of inlay are the most usual forms of decoration found on Chester County furniture. Perhaps the most notable characteristic is the decorative effect of a voluted inlay. The rural cabinet-maker having completed the case and desiring an embellishment, took a compass and scribed a series of interjoined volutes or half circles, terminating each volution with a group of inlaid berries. For a desk or chest of drawers this frequently became an over-all decoration on the front of the piece.

The light wood of the holly tree was used to fill the design, which had been carefully gouged out on the surface. It is interesting to note that some of the berry inlays terminate with two holly berries, and one cherry inlay berry to provide color and variety.

Herringbone inlay is another feature of Chester County inlaid furniture. Alternating diagonals of holly and cherry, and less often cedar wood, are made to fill a section of a drawer front or door of a spice box. Herringbone inlay is rarer than the berry and line inlay.

William and Mary walnut inlaid bible box marked "I E". Secondary wood pine. Height 9″, width 22 1/2″, depth 14 1/4″.
Mrs. Herbert F. Schiffer collection

William and Mary Wainscot walnut side chair having the typical
Chester County crest rail and line inlay on the back inset panel. Height
42″, seat height 17″, width 20″, depth 16″.

Chester County Historical Society collection

William and Mary walnut inlaid chest of drawers. The chest of drawers has line and berry inlay on top "I B 1706". This is the earliest piece of dated inlaid furniture found thus far. Secondary woods pine and poplar. Height 34 1/2″, width 30 1/2″, depth 21″.
Mrs. Herbert F. Schiffer collection

Detail of line and berry inlay. This chest of drawers is mentioned in the inventory of John Worrall, Nether Providence township taken on February 9, 1799, as "Little Old Bureau Markt I B 1706".

William and Mary inlaid blanket chest. The brass inlaid initials "C S" are for Cadwalader Supplee. Secondary wood pine. Height 27", width 50 1/2", depth 22 1/2".
Chester County Historical Society collection

William and Mary walnut gate leg table with line and berry inlay on the drop leaf. Marked "I E B 1725" for James and Elizabeth Bartram. Secondary woods oak and pine. Height 30 3/4", width 60", length 70".
William W. Wilson, Jr. collection

Detail of inlay on gate leg table.

William and Mary walnut inlaid desk. The desk has herringbone, line and berry and tulip inlay. Secondary woods, chestnut black locust, red cedar and tulip. Height 45 1/4″, width 39 1/4″, depth 22 1/8″.
Courtesy, The Henry Francis du Pont Winterthur Museum.

Queen Anne walnut inlaid bible box marked "H P 1739". Height 7 3/4", width 19", depth 14 1/4".
Chester County Historical Society collection

William and Mary walnut chest of drawers initialed and dated "M ^{M} L 1750". Secondary woods poplar and cedar. Height 43 1/2", width 40 1/2", depth 23 3/4".
Mrs. Herbert F. Schiffer collection

William and Mary walnut chest of drawers with line and berry inlay. Secondary woods pine and cedar. The inlay is holly and cherry. Height 37", width 40", depth 23".

Mrs. Herbert F. Schiffer collection

Detail showing the line inlay on the top of the chest of drawers.

Queen Anne walnut chest of Drawers. The chest of drawers has line and berry inlay and tulips. The secondary woods are tulip and chestnut. Height 49 1/8″, width 41 1/2″, depth 22 3/8″.

Courtesy, The Henry Francis du Pont Winterthur Museum.

Queen Anne walnut inlaid high chest of drawers. Secondary wood poplar. Height 59″, width 30 1/4″, depth 22″.

Mrs. Herbert F. Schiffer collection

Queen Anne walnut inlaid dresser. The dresser has inlay and initials on the two cupboard doors and an initial on the two top drawers. Secondary wood poplar. Height 78″, width 35 1/2″, depth 16″.

Mrs. Herbert F. Schiffer collection

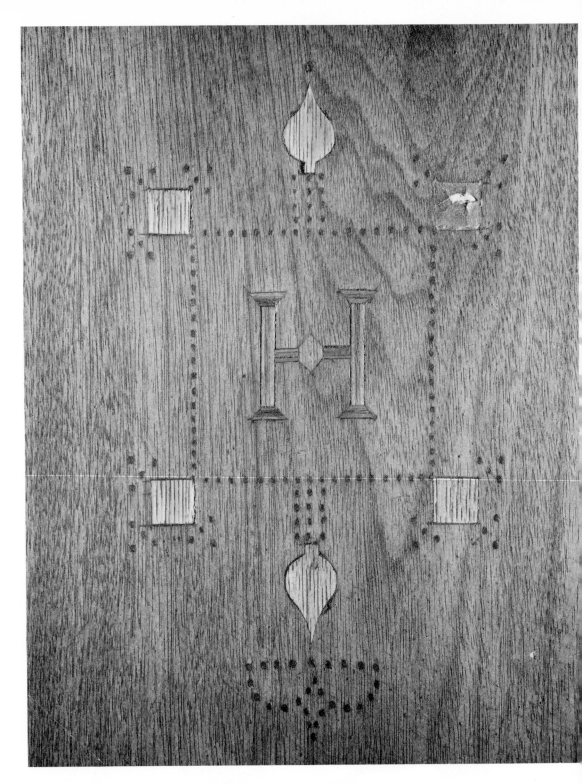

Inlay detail of Queen Anne dresser on previous page.

Queen Anne walnut inlaid blanket chest initialed and dated "SEP 1782". Secondary wood poplar. Height 25 1/2″, width 43″, depth 18 1/2″.

Mr. and Mrs. Peter B. Schiffer

Chippendale walnut inlaid tall case clock. Inscribed "B Chandlee Nottingham" (b. 1723, d. 1791 working East Nottingham township).

Secondary wood poplar. Height 80″.
Mrs. Herbert F. Schiffer collection

Detail of Chippendale Clock.

Chippendale walnut inlaid slant lid desk. Secondary wood poplar. Height 43 1/2″, writing height 32″, width 39″, depth 19 1/4″.

Mrs. Herbert F. Schiffer collection

WILLIAM AND MARY FURNITURE

The earliest Chester County furniture included the wainscot chair, settle and blanket chest. The blanket chests were characterized by the stile and rail construction, with panels set in, from which wainscot furniture received its name. Frequently they had small ball feet, but occasionally the stiles formed the feet.

WAINSCOT CHAIRS WITH CHESTER COUNTY CREST RAILS

Chairs of this type are among the earliest survivals in the Delaware Valley and seem almost medieval in design. The chair incorporates almost all the decorative devices employed by local chairmakers at the end of the seventeenth century; vigorously turned front posts and stretcher, kept within the plains of the block; shaped and scored arms with graceful under cutting; molded seat frame usually made to receive a cushion; semi-circular tops to rear posts; recessed or raised back panel; and an elaborate crest consisting of a central fan and two horns. This particular cresting has been found on numerous chairs made by an unknown Chester County joiner. In order of frequency the primary woods for chairs of this type are walnut, oak and cherry. More arm chairs have been found thus far than side chairs. Some chairs have inset balusters below the crest rail.

A particularly interesting Delaware Valley counterpart of New England's Pilgrim century bannister back furniture is this arm chair. The half circle crest rail is a structural feature widely used in the Delaware Valley area. However, when it is decorated with punched stars it becomes quite local. The forms found having the star decoration are arm chairs and day beds, all with rush seats. The usual wood used in construction was maple. The chairs and day beds were usually painted black. It is probable that the star decorated furniture originated between Chester, Pennsylvania and New Castle, Delaware — a twenty mile area.

Walnut baluster back side chair with Chester County crest rail. Height 40", seat height 17", width 18 1/2", depth 15".

Chester County Historical Society collection

Walnut banister back arm chair. Height 45 1/2", seat height 16", width 22", depth 18".

Mrs. Herbert F. Schiffer collection

Walnut banister back side chair. Height 45 1/2", seat height 19", width 18 1/2", depth 14".

Mrs. Herbert F. Schiffer collection

Baluster back painted arm chair with star punched decoration. Poplar and maple woods. Height 45", seat height 18", width 21 1/2", depth 18".
Mrs. Herbert F. Schiffer collection

Wainscot arm chair with Chester County crest rail. Height 44 1/2″, seat height 17″, width 25″, depth 18″.
Titus C. Geesey collection

Detail of the back of the baluster back painted arm chair showing the star punched decoration.

Walnut settle attributed to Abraham Darlington. Inlaid initials and date "17 I E P 58" for Isaac and Elizabeth Pyle. Elizabeth was Abraham Darlington's sister. Height 53", width 71", depth 21".

Chester County Historical Society collection

Maple day bed. Height 14 1/2", height of back 49 1/4", length 68", depth 24".

Chester County Historical Society collection

Walnut clothes press. Height 78 1/2", width 41 1/2", depth 23".
Chester County Historical Society collection

Walnut desk on frame. Secondary woods pine and oak. Height 41″, writing height 35″, width 32 1/2″, depth 25 1/2″.
Titus C. Geesey collection

Walnut desk on frame. Secondary woods poplar and white cedar. Height 42 1/2″, writing height 33″, width 37″, depth 20 1/4″.

Mrs. Herbert F. Schiffer collection

Oak desk. Secondary wood cedar. Height 39″, width 37″, depth 21″.
Chester County Historical Society collection

Walnut stretcher base table. Height 29″, width 18″, depth 17″.
Mrs. Herbert F. Schiffer collection

Walnut stretcher base table with drawer. Secondary woods poplar and pine. Height 27 1/2″, width 37 1/2″, depth 28 1/4″.
Mrs. Herbert F. Schiffer collection

Walnut joint stool. Height 25″, width 20″, depth 14″.
Chester County Historical Society collection

Walnut stretcher base table. Height 26 1/2″, diameter of top 22 1/4″.
Mrs. Herbert F. Schiffer collection

Walnut stretcher base table with drawer. Height 27″, width 29 1/2″,
depth 19 1/2″.
Mrs. Herbert F. Schiffer collection

Walnut stretcher base table with drawer. Secondary woods pine and
white cedar. Height 28 1/4″, width 32″, depth 22 1/4″.
Mrs. Herbert F. Schiffer collection

1794 Taufschein attributed to Jacob Oberholtzer. It was made for Maria Emrich in Pikeland township, Chester county. 6 5/16″ by 4″.
Mrs. Herbert F. Schiffer collection

Walnut dressing table. Secondary woods pine and white cedar. Height 25″, width 36″, depth 23 1/2″.

Mrs. Herbert F. Schiffer collection

Walnut dressing table. Secondary wood poplar. Height 30", width 35", depth 21".
Mrs. Herbert F. Schiffer collection

Walnut arm chair. Height 40 1/2", seat height 17", width 23", depth 18 1/2".
Mrs. Herbert F. Schiffer collection

Walnut high chest of drawers. Secondary wood poplar. The feet are removable. Height 62", width 28", depth 20 3/4".

Mrs. Herbert F. Schiffer collection

Walnut drop leaf dining table. Secondary wood oak. Height 28 1/2",
width 48 1/2", length 58".

Mrs. Herbert F. Schiffer collection

Miniature paper and wood bed. Found in a shell and wax works.
Height 5", length 4 1/2", depth 3".

Chester County Historical Society collection

Walnut clothes press. Secondary woods poplar and white cedar. Height
74 3/4", width 44 1/2", depth 17 1/4".
Mrs. Herbert F. Schiffer collection

left Six slat side chair with rush seat. Woods maple and chestnut. Height 45 1/2″, seat height 18″, width 19″, depth 15″.
Mrs. Herbert F. Schiffer collection

right Five slat side chair with rush seat. Woods maple and chestnut. Height 44 1/2″, seat height 17 1/2″, width 18 1/4″, depth 15″.
Mrs. Herbert F. Schiffer collection

Open pine hanging shelves. Height 45".
Mrs. Herbert F. Schiffer collection

Hanging walnut cupboard. Secondary wood tulip poplar. Height 31 3/8", width 22 5/8", depth 11".
Mrs. Herbert F. Schiffer collection

Maple slant lid desk. Secondary woods pine and poplar. Height 42 1/2″, writing height 31″, width 38″, depth 22″.

Chester County Historical Society collection

Walnut spice box on frame. Height 34″, width 18″, depth 9″.
Anonymous

CHIPPENDALE FURNITURE

OCTORARA FURNITURE

The chest of drawers stands on removable feet. They are permanently attached to a batten that runs from front to back. The two battens are fastened to the case by two removable wooden screws. The heads of the screws protrude below the battens. If these wooden screws are removed the battens with the attached legs can be removed.

The Octorara desk is a distinctive local form found along the creek of this name, which forms the western boundary of Chester County. The typical desk has these special features: high, full ogee feet with a closed circle cut out, plain (rather than reeded or fluted) quarter columns, and so-called "pen" or "candle" drawers for the fall front writing surface usually made of oak with a facing (these facings each contain an intaglio carved pinwheel), shaped interior drawers, pigeon hole side panels, and shell carved pigeon hole drawers and central door. The desks are usually of walnut with oak, pine and poplar as secondary woods.

High chests of drawers, usually of walnut, having the plain quarter column and the high ogee foot with a closed circle cut out, two of the Octorara characteristics are known. Less frequently chests on chests, clothes presses, clock and blanket chests are found.

previous page

Walnut arm chair. Height 39 1/4", seat height 15 1/4", width 25 1/2", depth 18 1/4".
Chester County Historical Society collection

Transitional walnut side chairs. (Left) Height 40″, seat height 17 1/2″, width 20″, depth 16 1/4″. (Right) Height 40″, seat height 17″, width 20 1/2″, depth 16 1/2″.
Mrs. Herbert F. Schiffer collection

right Walnut tilt top candlestand. Height 29″, diameter of top 30″. Signed "Beidler" (Jacob Beidler, b. 1778, d. 1864. Working in East Whiteland township).
Mrs. Herbert F. Schiffer collection

Walnut slant lid desk. Signed "Robt. Eachus" (working in East Caln township ca. 1763). Secondary woods are white oak, poplar and cedar. Height 42 1/4″, writing height 29 1/4″, width 35 3/4″, depth 21 1/4″.
Mrs. Herbert F. Schiffer collection

Interior of walnut slant lid desk.

"Robt. Eachus" signature.

Octorara walnut high chest of drawers. Secondary wood poplar. Height 69 1/2″, width 39 1/2″, depth 21″.

Mr. and Mrs. Pusey J. Singer collection

Walnut desk and bookcase. Secondary woods pine and poplar. Height
91″, writing height 32″, width 50″, depth 23″.
Chester County Historical Society collection

Octorara walnut slant lid desk. Secondary wood pine. Height 47 1/4″,
writing height 35″, width 41″, depth 21 1/2″.
Chester County Historical Society collection

Walnut Pembroke table. Secondary woods pine and poplar. Height
27 3/4″, width 40″, depth 29 1/2″.
Chester County Historical Society collection

Octorara painted blanket chest. Height 23″, width 50″, depth 23″.

Octorara walnut high chest of drawers. Secondary woods poplar and chestnut. Height 71″, width 44″, depth 32″.

Mrs. Herbert F. Schiffer collection

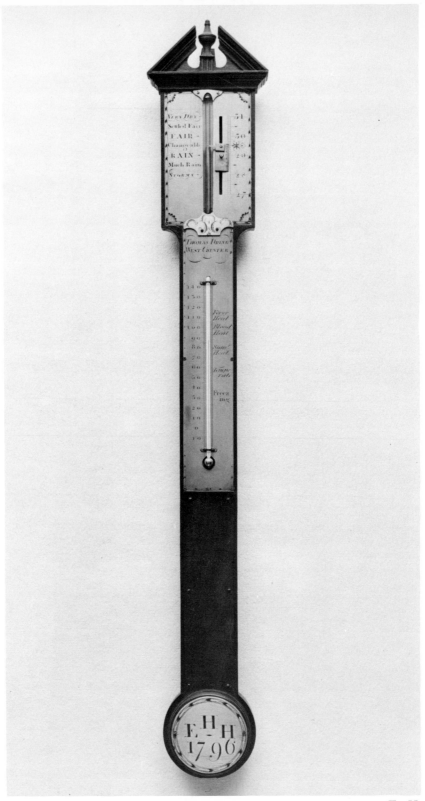

Walnut barometer. Signed "Thomas Dring West Chester E H H
[Edward and Hannah Hicks] 1796". Height 39″, width 6 1/2″.
Dial is silver washed and the finial is brass.

Chester County Historical Society collection

CLASSICAL FURNITURE

Hepplewhite mahogany card table with satinwood inlay marked "S. T. BELLERJEAU". He worked as a cabinet-maker in West Chester between 1823 and 1825 and in East Caln township in 1826 and 1827. Height 29 3/4", width 37 3/4", depth 18 1/2", depth open 37".
Courtesy Henry Francis du Pont Winterthur Museum

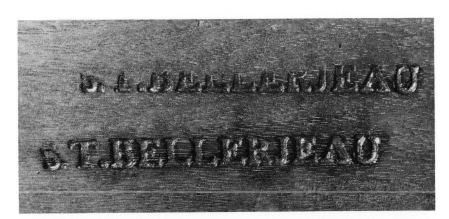

Mahogany veneered and inlaid chest of drawers. Labelled "Isaac Weaver". He worked in West Chester 1805 to 1813. Secondary wood poplar. Height 38″, width 42″, depth 19 1/2″.

Chester County Historical Society collection

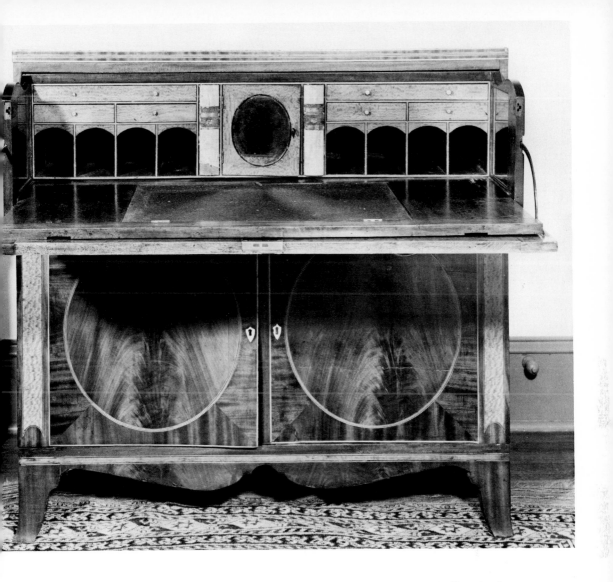

Mahogany veneered and inlaid fall front desk. Signed "made by Thomas Dilworth 1801". He worked in Chester county between 1801 and 1805. Secondary wood poplar, maple inlay. Height 41 1/4″, writing height 29 1/2″, width 42 1/2″, depth 20 1/4″.

Mr. and Mrs. Francis E. Judson collection

Painted bamboo turned side chair. Pine, poplar and maple woods. Label under seat of Burchall and Wickersham who worked in West Chester between 1822 and 1824. Height 34″, seat height 16 1/2″, width 16″, depth 16″.

Mrs. Herbert F. Schiffer collection

WINDSOR FURNITURE

Windsor candlestands are the county's contribution to the field of Windsor furniture. They have circular tops supported by three turned legs and braced by three turned stretchers. They average twenty-five inches in height. and the circular dish top averages seventeen inches in diameter The turnings vary from the bold Windsor turnings of 1760-1770 to the bamboo turnings of about 1800. The earliest candle-stands found are constructed of walnut or butternut wood and were not painted. Later stands were made of soft woods, had bamboo turnings and were painted either red or green.

Painted arrow back arm chairs. Label under seat of Joseph Jones who worked in West Chester between 1817 and 1846. Poplar and hickory woods. Height 33 1/2″, seat height 18″, width 19″, depth 17″.
Chester County Historical Society collection

Painted child's arm chair marked on the bottom of seat "From Abm Sharpless to James Massey 1800 Take good care of this." He worked in Concord township in 1771. Height 23", seat height 10 1/4", width 12", depth 10 1/2".

Bow back arm chair branded under seat "CUSTER." Jesse Custer worked in 1796 in Vincent township and Coventry township in 1771. Height 23", seat height 10 1/4", width 12", depth 10 1/2".

Mrs. Herbert F. Schiffer collection

Spinning wheel marked "J. SUGAR". He worked in West Bradford Township.

Chester County Historical Society collection

Walnut candlestand. Height 25″, diameter of dished top 18 1/2″.
Mrs. Herbert F. Schiffer collection

Cradle marked "I LETCHWORTH". He worked in East Fallowfield township in 1823 and 1824. The cradle was made for Mary Downing Valentine wife of George Valentine, iron master. Height 26 1/2″, width 17 1/2″, length 34″.
Chester County Historical Society collection

Painted pine Sheraton blanket chest signed on bottom of drawer "Anselom Moore". He appears as a cabinetmaker in the Charlestown township tax assessment for 1821. Height 29 1/4″, width 48″, depth 19″.

Hibernia collection

Walnut drop leaf table labelled "G. R. JOHNSON, CABINET MAKER
& UNDERTAKER GAY ST., SOUTH SIDE BETWEEN CHURCH
AND DARLINGTON, WEST CHESTER, PA. FASHIONABLE AND
WELL MADE FURNITURE CONSTANTLY ON HAND. RECORD
PRINTER." George R. Johnson worked in West Chester in 1850.
Height 28 3/4", width 51", depth 38".
Joseph Reeder collection

Mahogany veneered wash stand with marble top labelled "FROM JAMES CHALFANT Cabinet Maker, Unionville, Pa." He worked in East and West Marlboro townships between 1829 and 1857. Secondary woods pine and poplar. Height 36″, width 26″, depth 18″.
Hibernia collection

Mahogany veneered sewing table labelled "FROM JAMES CHAL-FANT Cabinet Maker, Unionville, Pa." He worked in East and West Marlboro townships between 1829 and 1857. Secondary woods poplar and pine. Height 28″, width 23″, depth 16 1/2″.
Hibernia collection

Mahogany veneered chest of drawers labelled "FROM JAMES CHAL-
FANT Cabinet Maker, Unionville, Pa." He worked in East and West
Marlboro townships between 1829 and 1857. Secondary woods pine
and poplar. Height 43 1/2", width 47 1/2", depth 23".
Hibernia collection

BOXES

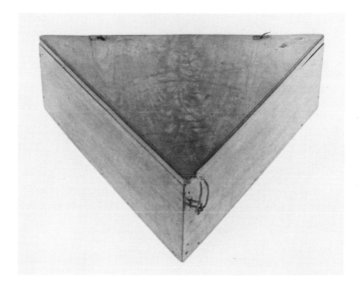

Walnut hat box. 18 1/2″ each side.
Mrs. Herbert F. Schiffer collection

Wall paper hat box. The inside is lined with a copy of *The American Republican and Chester County Democrat,* West Chester, Pa., Tuesday May 17, 1842. Height 9″.
Mrs. Herbert F. Schiffer collection

Queen Anne walnut tall case clock. Inscribed "B. Chandlee, Nottingham". Benjamin Chandlee worked in Nottingham township between 1718 and 1740. Secondary wood chestnut. Height 84″. Surmounting the sarcophagus hood is a crest with two painted love birds.
Chester County Historical Society collection

Chippendale walnut tall case clock. Documented case made by Jacob Brown who worked in West Nottingham township between 1788 and 1797. Works by Benjamin Chandlee, Jr. (b. 1723, d. 1791), working in East Nottingham township. Secondary wood oak. Height 80".
Mrs. J. Norman McDowell collection

Classical cherry tall case clock. The clock case is marked "I WEAVER". Isaac Weaver worked in West Chester between 1805 and 1813. The works are by Jacob Urich of Wilmington. Height 93".
Anonymous

William and Mary walnut inlaid spice box. Secondary woods poplar and chestnut. Height 19″, width 16″, depth 10 3/4″.

SPICE BOXES

Spice boxes were made in Chester county from the end of the seventeenth century to the early part of the nineteenth century, and consequently the same motifs employed by the cabinet makers on their full size furniture were used on these diminutive pieces. They were used to hold small articles of value such as silver spoons, silver and gold buttons and silver banded pin cushions. Spice boxes rest on ball feet, bracket feet (straight, cut out, full ogee and French); or on frames with trumpet turned, Spanish, pointed slipper and claw and ball feet. All local spice cabinets have a door with a lock. Sometimes only the door has inlaid decoration, in other instances this inlay is also found on the sides, interior drawers and rather seldom on the top. The "secret" compartment when found in spice boxes is in the cornice, in the back panel or in back of front drawers. One spice box with quarter columns and one with a bow front are known. The woods employed were walnut, cherry, apple, mahogany, maple, cedar, poplar and butternut.

In 1715 Richard Fletcher, in Kennett township made a "spice box and 2 coffins 4:13:0".

The inventory of Jacob Hibberd in 1750 lists the contents of his spice box.

To one Spice Box Sundreys therein

To 2 links of Gold Sleeve Buttons 2 links of Silver ditto & 2 Silver studds

To a pair of Silver shoe Clasps 1 pr Brass ditto

To 1 Pin Cussion with a Silver belt and Chain

To a Silver Scizars Chain and thimble of ditto

To 2 Large Silver spoons 6 Silver Tea spoons and one pair of Silver Tongs

To Sundrey Small things.

William and Mary cedar inlaid spice box. The spice box has line inlay on door, top, sides and interior drawers. Secondary woods oak and pine. Height 18 1/2", width 18", depth 10".
Mrs. Herbert F. Schiffer collection

Inlay detail of William and Mary's Spice Box.

Queen Anne walnut spice box on frame. The spice box has herring-bone and line and berry inlay. Height 26 1/2″, width 16 1/4″, depth 11 1/2″.

Courtesy, The Henry Francis du Pont Winterthur Museum.

Queen Anne walnut inlaid spice box. The spice box has herringbone and line and berry inlay on the door and sides which is rarely found. Secondary wood pine. Height 23 1/2″, width 16 1/2″, depth 19 1/2″.

Gunsmiths

Chester county had a number of gunsmiths. The following men are listed in public records as gunsmiths: 1775 Joel Bailey in West Bradford township; 1811, 1812 and 1813 Adam Yeager in Pikeland township; 1811 William Rentken in Pikeland township; 1819 Patrick Little in Sadsbury township; 1825 George Winters in East Caln township and in 1842 Jacob Baker in West Chester, Emmer Fling in East Bradford township, Jacob Gilbo in East Fallowfield township, Jacob Knauer, Nathan Morey and Thomas Vanderslice in Schuylkill township.

In 1821 "Levi Jackson, Respectfully informs his friends and the public that he has commenced the Gunsmith Business High Street, a few doors below Mr. Babb's tavern, where he will execute all orders confided to him, with punctuality and despatch. He makes Rifles, Muskets, Shot guns and Pistols: and does every thing in his line of business. He hopes by attention to business and the goodness of his work to merit and obtain the patronage of a generous public."[1]

In 1830 Em'l Goulcher advertised:

GUN-MAKING

THE subscriber begs leave to return his very sincere thanks to the inhabitants of West-Chester, and the public at large for the liberal encouragement he has been favoured with, since his commencing business in this Borough, and hopes by continued exertions to merit their extended approbation.

Gun-Making and Repairing, in all its branches; Guns Percussioned in the best possible manner; likewise Door and Cabinet Locks repaired; Keys fitted, and general Smith Jobbing. For Sale-Double and Single Guns, Shot Belts, Powder Flasks, Powder Horns and Game Bags, Wad Cutters, Bullet Moulds and Percussion Caps-Shot and Powder of the best quality—by

EM'L GOULCHER[2]

---

[1] *Village Record*, West Chester, Pa., May 16, 1821.

[2] Ibid., November 10, 1830.

Metals

COPPER

The following men are listed as coppersmiths in the public records.

Apple, Edward	West Chester	1842
Apple, William	West Chester	1830-1849
Entriken, George	Goshen Twp.	1799
Gilbert, James	Phoenixville	1844
Greham, Francis	Goshen Twp.	1799
Headona, Andrew	Sadsbury Twp.	1842
Lent, William	West Chester & Downingtown	1828
	West Chester	1829
	East Caln Twp.	1842
Northrop, William	East Caln Twp.	1842
Rettew, John, Jr.	Goshen Twp.	1797-1801
	West Chester	1803-1804
	Goshen Twp.	1807

Copper sun dial marked "Philip Roman Fecit 1726". Roman worked in Chichester at that time, a part of Chester County. The inventory of his estate taken in 1729 lists a copper furnace. Diameter 5".
Chester County Historical Society collection

CUTLERS

The following men are listed as cutlers in the public records.

Baldwin, Joshua	East Caln Twp.	1747-1765
Bolton, George	Springfield Twp.	1788
Cope, David	West Nottingham Twp.	1778-1797
Cope, Jonathan	East Bradford Twp.	1802-1807
Garratt, William	Darby Twp.	1768
Gill, David	Charlestown Twp.	1799
Gill, George	Goshen Twp.	1785
Haines, John	Honey Brook Twp.	1810-1818
Hartt, John	East Caln Twp.	1762
	West Caln Twp.	1771
Hibberd, John	Darby Twp.	1784
Hibbon, Thomas	West Caln Twp.	1788
Jones, Benjamin	Tredyffrin Twp.	1782-1783
Jones, James	West Nottingham Twp.	1803
	East Nantmeal Twp.	1804
Kinsey, Ulysses	West Caln Twp.	1802
Lownes, Curtis	Springfield Twp.	1788
Lownes, George	Middletown & Springfield Twps.	1781
Lownes, Slater	Middletown & Springfield Twps.	1781-1782
		1830
Maule, Ebenezer	West Fallowfield Twp.	1782-1794
Oglesby, George	West Caln Twp.	1811-1820
	Sadsbury Twp.	1813-1818
Oglesby, Jonah	Sadsbury Twp.	1813-1818
Oglesby, Joseph	Sadsbury Twp.	1785
Penington, Thomas	London Grove Twp.	1789
Sowalter, Ulrich	Londonderry Twp.	

GOLDSMITHS

Three men have been found working as goldsmiths in the county.

Benjamin Chandlee

Benjamin Chandlee, a clockmaker is mentioned as a silversmith in the tax assessment for East Nottingham Township in 1770 and as a goldsmith in the same township in 1774.

Aaron Musgrave, Jr.

In 1794 Aaron Musgrave advertised:

Aaron Musgrave, Jr.
Gold and Silver Smith
CONTINUES to carry on the above business, in the town of West Chester in all its various branches, and makes and sells on the lowest terms, Silver Tea pots, Sugar bowles, Canns and Cream-pots, soup ladles, table and tea spoons, sugar tongs, pincushion hoopes and chains, scisars, chains, spurs, shoe, knee, stock, boot and hat buckles, coat jacket and sleeve buttons, broaches, thimbles, and shoe clasps, gold lockets breast pins twist set and plain gold rings, sleeve buttons, stock buckles and breeches &c. &c.

He has now on hand, a neat assortment of silver ware, and will make any thing in his line of business upon short notice; and warrants his silver equal in fineness to Spanish dollars, and his work he hopes upon examination and trial will recommend itself. He has also for sale, a variety of fashionable plate and metal shoe and knee buckles, plated spurs, steel and gilt seals and keys, penknives, pocketbooks, razors and straps together with a variety of other articles. — and also for sale at the same place on very [   ] terms, mens and womens hats, and a few dozen pair of womens white kid gloves.
N.B. An Apprentice wanted at the above business.[1]

WILLIAM RATTEW

The will of Thomas Baldwin, of Chester Township, reads in part "Chester July the Second 1731 Then personally appeared Wm. Rattew Goldsmith. . ."[2]

---

[1]*West Chester Gazette,* (West Chester, Pa.), Jan. 8, 1794.

[2] *Chester County Will Book 1,* p. 335.

PEWTER

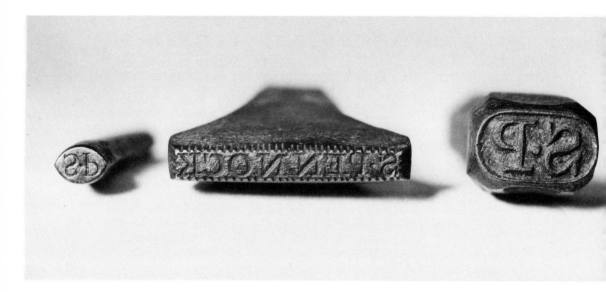

Dies used by Samuel and Simon Pennock.
Chester County Historical Society collection

The following men (with birth and death dates), worked as pewterers in the county:

Isaac Jackson	1732-1807	New Garden Twp.
Elisha Kirk	1757-1790	New Garden Twp.
David Lamborn	1764-1855	London Grove Twp.
Samuel Pennock	1754-1843	East Marlboro Twp.
Simon Pennock	1781-1868	East Marlboro Twp.
Robert Porter	? -1785	East Caln Twp.

Pewter soup bowl and tureen used at Westtown School. Soup bowl height 2″, diameter 5 1/2″. Tureen, height 8″, diameter 13″.
Chester County Historical Society collection

Pewter porringers made by Samuel and Simon Pennock.
Chester County Historical Society collection

Robert Porter
1785 Vendue of Robert Porter

The Condition of this Present Vendue held at the House of Robert Valentine Junr. this 22nd of the 12th month 1785. of the Goods and Effects of Robert Porter Deceased, are that the Highest Bidder shall be the Buyer, any Person buying to the amount of thirty Shillings or upwards shall have three Months Credit upon giving Security if required, and all Sums under thirty Shillings to be ready Money, and any person Buying to the amount of thirty Shillings or more and Neglecting to give Security as aforesaid shall be held to Prisent Pay.

by Thos. Pim, Exr.

		£	s	d
Robert Valentine Jr.	To a Hatchet		2	1
Thomas Shugar	2 Augers		2	0
Rich'd Robinson	2 Squares		1	0
Thos. Shugar	a Chisel & gouge		1	2
Robt Miller	Do		1	8
Isaac Webb	2 Screw Augers		3	9
Robt Valentine	Adds		5	6
Jonathan Parke	4 Sash Chisels		1	11
Thos Shugar	3 Do		0	10
Robt Miller	Plain & Gage		0	7
George Valentine	Chisel		2	0
Robert Miller	2 Drawing-knives		2	3
Joseph Hinnison	Brace & hammer		1	8
Jonathan Parke	Schrew box & lap		1	1
Wm Trimble	Frough		2	3
Robt Valentine	Saw		1	0
Wm Mills	Spoke Shave & Sundries		1	0
Robt Valentine	3 Plains		1	7
Ditto	Jointer		4	2
Jonathan Parke	Plain & Cumposes		2	11
Joseph Green	2 Hammers		2	3
Jonathan Parke	Gage & Schrew Cutter		0	7
Isaac Webb	Broad Ax		2	2
John Edge	Drill		0	6
Abraham Simcox	2 Grindstone Cranks		2	1
Paul Kester	Soudering Irons & Ladle		1	1
Rich'd Robinson	Bench hook & Sundries		1	2
Abm Simcox	Nail tool		0	7
Isaac Webb	Basket		1	1
Wm Mills	Gun	1	0	0
		3 . 11 .	11	
Robt Valentine	Powder-horn & Shotbag		3	0
Thos Pim Jur	Knife		1	7
Abraham Simcox	Vise	1	0	0
John Hughs	Schrew plate		2	1
Joel Davis	Bucket		1	7
Robert Valentine Jur	Kettle		2	0
Jonathan Parke	Tennant Saw		4	1
Ditto	Taper bit & Sundries		1	1
Wm Whittaker	Tennant Saw		5	1

		£	S	d
Joel Davis	Hand Saw		9	6
Joseph Carpenter	3 Plains		0	6
Joel Davis	Box of Sundries		1	8
Robt Woodward	3 files		0	7
John Edge	Nippers & pliers		0	6
John Keragin	2 Cornish Prisms		2	7
John Hughs	Saws & files		1	6
Ditto	Trencher & Sundries		1	6
Paul Kester	Shaveing box & Sundries		1	0
Thos Stalker Senr	Screw & Sundries		1	0
Griffh Mendenhall	Plain bits & sundries		1	9
Jonathan Parke	Schrew & sundries		1	1
Thos Pim Senr	Scales & sundries		2	6
Wm Mills	Sundries		3	4
Griffh Mendenhall	Ledd		2	7
Wm Whitaker	3 Plains		2	4
Thos Hollis	3 Do		0	7
Thos Cleark	4 Do		1	1
John Herragin	6 Do		1	1
Wm Whitaker	2 Do		4	1
John Hoops	1 Do		0	7
Robt Woodward	Wooden Schrew		0	6
John Whitaker	Grindstone & Wheel		17	11
Robt Valentine Jur	Turning Machine	2	14	0
Abiah Parke	Porenger Molds	2	10	0
Robt Valentine Jur	3 Turning Chissels		3	9
John Hoops	5 Turning Hooks			
	Borenger Mold Soap stone		3	9
John Hoops	a Pair Bellows	1	5	3
Thos Gheen Jur	Bason & Sundries		2	3
Thos Green	Saddle	1	0	0
Abm Simcox	Whetstone		1	0
John Hoops	Combe works		3	1
John Edge	2 Wooden porrengers		1	5
		13 .	4 .	9
Wm Mills	a pr Cloggs		2	0
Ditto	8 Plates 1/8 pr piece		13	4
John Hoops	6 Porengers 1/8 Do		10	0
John Buchannan	18 1/4 Linnen by yd 2/10	2	11	8
Thos Pim Junr	6 Porrengers 1/9 pr piece		10	6
Wm Mills	6 Do 2/		12	0
Jesse Evans	6 Do 1/9		10	6
Griffth Mendenhall	6 Do by Lump		6	11
Wm Mills	6 Do pr piece 1/10		11	0
Richd Robinson	6 Do Do 1/10		11	0
Wm Whitaker	3 Do Do 1/11		5	9
Joshua Weaver	Shaving Box & strap		0	7
Thos Cleark	Book		1	7
Do	Do		1	7
Do	Law Do		3	5
Joel Davis	Brush		4	0
Wm Mills	2 Raisorw & soap		4	6
Thos Stalker Senr	Shaving Box		1	1

		£	S	d
Wm Tremble	Cork Schrew	1	1	
Robt Valentine Jur	2 Maps	0	6	
Michael Buchannan	2 Glass & Phial	1	9	
Thos Green	Horn Tumbler	1	9	
John Edge	Thread	2	0	
Thos Pim Jur	Horn Tumbler	1	0	
James Keimer	2 Watch Springs & Sundries	1	3	
Joshua Roman	Powder horn	3	0	
Do	Hat	6	9	
John Edge	Yarn & Sundries	1	1	
Thos Johnston	Plane	1	0	
George Valentine	Inkhorn & Sundries	1	2	
Jame Keimer	Plain bit	0	2	
Robt Valentine Jur	Book	1	7	
Joseph Kinneson	Pipe & Sundries		4	
Joshua Roman	Pocket Books		2	
Joseph Green	Book	2	11	
Thos Gheen Jur	Do	2	1	

11 . 10 . 6

The Vendue of the Goods and Effects of Robert Porter, Deceased, held on January 22, 1785 listed the following items sold:

	£	S	d
To a hatchet		2	1
2 Augers		2	0
2 Squares		1	0
a Chessel gouge		1	2
Do		1	8
2 Screw Augers		3	9
Adds		5	6
2 Sash Chissels		1	11
3 Do		0	10
Plain & Gage		0	7
Chissel		2	0
2 Drawing knives		2	3
Brace & hammer		1	8
Screw box & top		1	1
Trough		2	3
Saw		1	0
Shoke Shave & /sundries		1	0
3 Plains		1	7
Jointer		4	2
Plain & Cumpasses		2	11
2 Hammers		2	3
Gage & Schrew Cutter		0	7
Broad Ax		2	2
Drill		0	6
2 Grindstone Cranks		2	1
Soudering Irons & Ladle		1	1
Bench hook & sundries		1	2
Nail tool		0	7
2 Do		4	1
1 Do		0	7
Wooden Schrew		0	6

	£	S	d
Grindstone & Wheels		17	11
Turning Machine	2	14	0
Porenger Molds	2	10	0
3 Turning Chissels		3	9
5 Turning Hooks		3	9
Porenger Mold Soap stone			
a Pair Bellows	1	5	3
Bason & Sundries		2	3
Saddle	1	0	0
Whetstone		1	0
Combe works		3	1
2 Wooden porrengers		1	5
A Pr Cloggs		2	0
8 Plates 1/8 pr piece		13	4
6 Porengers 1/8 Do		10	0
18 1/4 Yds Linnen by Yd 2/10	2	11	8
6 Porrengers 1/9 Pr piece		10	6
6 Do 2/		12	0
6 Do 1/9		10	6
6 Do by Lump		6	11
6 Do Pr piece 1/10		11	0
6 Do Do 1/10		11	0
3 Do Do 1/11		5	9
Shaving Box & strap		0	7
Book		1	7
Do		1	1
Law Do		3	5
Bssket		1	1
Gun	1	0	0
Powder horn & Shotbag		3	0
Knife		1	7
Vise	1	0	0
Schrew plate		2	1
Bucket		1	7
Kettle		2	0
Tennant Saw		4	1
Taper bit & Sundries		1	1
Tennant Saw		5	1
Hand Saw		9	6
3 Plains		0	6
Box of Sundries		1	8
3 files		0	7
Nippers & pliers		0	6
2 Cornish Plains		2	7
Saws & files		1	6
Trencher & Sundries		1	6
HSaveing box & Sundries		1	0
Schrew & Sundries		1	0
Plain bits & Sundries		1	9
Schrew & Sundries		1	1
Scales & Sundries		2	6
Sundries		3	4
Ledd		2	7
3 Plains		2	4

	£	S	d
3 Do		0	7
4 Do		1	1
6 Do		1	1
Brush		4	0
2 Raisors & Soap		4	6
Shaving box		1	1
Cork Schrew		1	1
2 Maps		0	6
2 Glass & Phial		1	9
Horn Tumbler		1	9
Thread		2	0
Horn Tumpler		1	0
2 Watch Springs & Sundries		1	5
Powder horn		3	0
Hat	2	6	9
Yarn & Sundries		1	1
Plane		1	0
Inkhorn & Sundries		1	2
Plain bit		0	2
Book		1	7
Pipe & Sundries			4
Pocket Books			2
Book		2	11
Do		2	1
The total value of the Goods and Effects was	L11	10	6.

[1]Ms. #13612, *Chester County Historical Society collection.*

SILVER

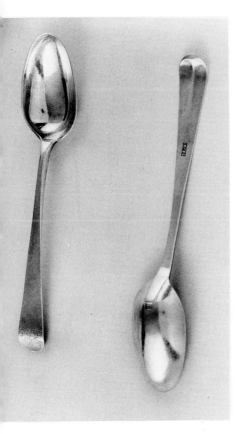

Tea spoons marked on the back "J L T". John Le Telier worked in West Marlboro township between 1795 and 1798.

Chester County Historical Society collection

Spoons and butter knives marked on the back "E. M. Bartlett West Chester." E. M. Bartlett worked in West Chester between 1834 and 1846.

Chester County Historical Society collection.

Spoons marked on the back "A M" and scissor hook marked "J. Brinton 1795." Aaron Musgrave worked in West Chester in 1794.
Chester County Historical Society collection

Tea spoons and sugar tongs marked "J. Weaver." Joshua Weaver worked in West Chester during the 1790's.
Chester County Historical Society collection

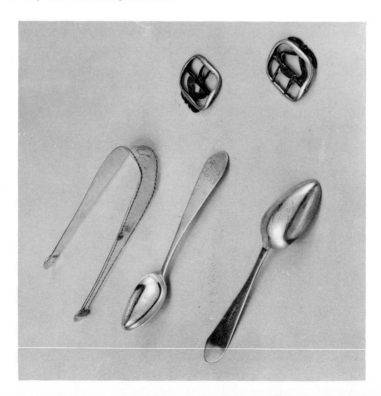

SILVER SMITHS

Taylor Allison

In 1841 Taylor Allison advertised:

Taylor Allison

CLOCK AND WATCH MAKING. THE subscriber very respectfully informs his friends and the public in general, that he has commenced the above business, at Doe Run, opposite Hayes Clark's Inn, and is prepared to repair all kinds of clocks and watches, musical boxes, accordions, jewelry and silver work in the best manner, at the shortest notice and on reasonable terms. Having employed Mr. Wm. R. Thomas, a first rate workman, he hopes to give general satisfaction to all who may favor him with a call. He has on hand a complete assortment of eight-day and thirty hour brass and brass bushed CLOCKS of a very superior quality, which he will sell reasonable and warrant to keep good time.

As his clocks are of the best manufacture and have been put in the best running order, persons wishing to purchase would do well to call and examine before going elsewhere. Chains, seals, watches and musical keys, pencils, finger rings, breast pins, and all articles usually kept in the above line. He hopes by strict attention to business and a desire to please to merit a liberal share of public patronage. Work warranted.

TAYLOR ALLISON [1]

William Baily

William Baily appears as a silversmith in the East Caln Township tax assessment for 1814. In the same year he advertised:

NOTICE.

I inform my friends and the public generally, that I have commenced business in DOWNINGTOWN, in the Clock & Watchmaking line, AND Silver Work; Where by punctuality and good workmanship, I hope to merit public patronage.

An assortment of watch chains, keys, seals &c. will constantly be kept on hand.

WILLIAM BAILY, JUN. [2]

In 1832 William Baily advertised:

WATCHES, JEWELLERY AND Silver Ware . . .[3]

George Baldwin

George Baldwin appears as a silversmith in the East Marlboro Township tax assessment for 1801.

George W. Baldwin

On April 3, 1837 George W. Baldwin of Sadsbury Township, silversmith, and Margaret, his wife sold a lot in West Fallowfield Township to Joseph Skelton, of Sadsbury Township.[4] George W. Baldwin was also a clock and watchmaker.[5]

Edward M. Bartlett

In 1834 Edward M. Bartlett and Henry W. Butler were working in West Chester in partnership. On September 9, 1834 they advertised:

Notice. The partnership heretofore existing between Henry W. Butler and Edward M. Bartlett, under the firm of Butler and Bartlett, is this day dissolved by mutual consent. All persons having claims against the firm are requested to present them for settlement, and all persons indebted to the firm are requested to present them for settlement, and all persons indebted to the firm are requested to make immediate payment to the said Edward M. Bartlett, who is duly authorized to settle the business of the firm.
HENRY W. BUTLER.
EDWARD M. BARTLETT.

The business will be carried on in future by the subscriber, who will always have on hand, the usual variety in his line.
EDWARD M. BARTLETT [6]

In October Edward M. Bartlett advertised:

Looking Glass, Jewelry, Silver Ware, and Fancy Hardware Store. EDWARD M. BARTLETT, BEGS leave to call public attention to his Stock of Goods, at the Store on Gay street, south side, a few doors west of the store of Mr. John W. Townsend. Here he offers for sale, on terms which economical purchasers cannot fail to appreciate:—
Looking Glasses, of various sizes, with gilt, mahogany and plainer frames; Brittannia Coffee Pots, Tea Pots, Sugar Bowls, Cream Jugs, Castors, 4, 5 and 6 bottles, &c. a very handsome assortment; Silver table Spoons, tea Spoons, Butter Knives, Thimbles, Bodkins, &c; Knives and Forks large and small Waiters, Candlesticks, Bread Baskets, Shaving Apparatus Complete; Straps, Spittoons, and a variety of necessary articles not named.
Clocks and Watches for sale, and the same neatly repaired on short notice.
E M B returns his sincere thanks to the former customers of Butler & Bartlett; and as their successor in business, he pledges himself to endeavor so to conduct his Shop as to be entitled to the public approbation.
N B SPECTACLES, with silver and steel Frames, constantly on hand; and a variety of Glasses, which will assist eyes of every age. Elderly friends, please to call. [7]

In 1835 he advertised:

WANTED AN Apprentice to the Silversmith business. An honest boy of industrious habits, well recommended, will be taken as an apprentice to the above business, if application be made soon. [8]

In 1836 as well as advertising what he sold Edward M. Bartlett advertised:

Wanted. A JOURNEYMAN SILVERSMITH and a good SPOON MAKER, constant employment and good wages will be given. [9]

In 1839 he advertised:

Silver Spoons, Watches Jewelry SPECTACLES, &c. THE subscriber continues to carry on the Watchmaking, Silversmith and Jewelry business, in West Chester. Clocks and Watches repaired at the shortest notice and warranted to perform well. He has on hand a good assortment of Silver Spoons, Spectacles of all kinds and prices, Jewelry, Thimbles Ever pointed Pencils Gold and Silver Watches and second hand do. As he manufactures his own silver work, persons wanting spoons, spectacles &c. will find they can obtain them as cheap if not cheaper than at Philadelphia; spectacle glasses to suit all ages. Thankful for the encouragement already given, he solicits a continuance of public patronage. [10]

In 1840 he advertised:

THE subscriber intending to remain in West Chester, one or two months perhaps, would be pleased to make (for those in want) silver spoons, spectacles, &c., or to repair everything in his line of business. He will be found at Grace's seed store, next door to Mr. Everhart's. [11]

Butler & Bartlett

Henry W. Butler and Edward M. Bartlett

Butler and Bartlett advertised in 1834:

Silver Spoon and Spectacles Manufactory. BUTLER & BARTLETT OPPOSITE the Cross Keys, West Chester, return their sincere thanks to the public for the liberal patronage already received, and invite attention to the following enumeration of articles, comprising an excellent assortment of NEW GOODS, just received such as mahogany framed Looking Glasses, fancy bellows, and hearth brushes, waiters, fancy shaving and dressing glasses, Britannia tea ware in sets, fine razors, penknives and scissors, eight day clocks, eight day brass time pieces, plated and fine Britannia castors, plated candlesticks, shaving brushes, razor straps and hones, silver thimbles, ever pointed pencils, scissors, hooks, knitting sheaths, fine snuffers and trays, together with a splendid assortment of Gold and Silver Watches and JEWELRY; spectacle glasses will be fitted to old frames to suit all ages, such as white, green, blue, conves, &c.

Clocks and watches carefully repaired according to order. Old gold and silver will be taken in exchange for any articles in their line. They respectfully solicit a continuance of public patronage, as their prices will be regulated by those of the Philadelphia market.[12] Removal. BUTLER & BARTLETT, Silversmiths, Jewellers, and WATCHMAKERS. HAVE removed from their former place, to that splendid store, formerly kept by Lewis Williams, in Gay street, three doors East of Messrs. Hoopes & Sharpless' store, where they still continue to manufacture silver table and tea spoons, spectacle and silver ware in general. In addition to their former stock of goods they have received a splendid assortment of fancy hardware, consisting of fine gilt, mahogany and common looking glasses, fancy toilet do. a splendid assortment of waiters, large and small, fine and common, knives and forks, fine penknives, scissors, raizors, snuffers and trays, brass and plated candle-sticks, shovels and tongs, brass andirons, japand lamps and candlesticks, bread trays, Dicksop's fine Britannia ware in sets, common do. do. fine and common castors, with 4, 5, 6 & 8 bottles, fancy brushes and bellows, snuff and tobacco boxes, razor straps, hones, soaps, and brushes, becket combs, perfumerv, lucifer matches, smelling bottles, silver and steel pens, silver and steel purses, clasps, bead purses, pins and needles, &c. &c.

Silver-ware and Jewellery.

Silver levers, English and French watches plated watch chains, seals, and keys, ear rings, finger rings, and breast pins, silver ever pointed pencils, silver table and tea spoons, plated do. do. scissors, hooks, knitting sheaths, fancy waste buckles, steel chains, bead gard chains, corral beads, &c. &c. spectacle glasses will be fitted to old frames to suit all ages, such as white, green, blue, conves, &c. . .[13]

Notice. The partnership heretofore existing between Henry W. Butler and Edward M. Bartlett, under the firm of Butler and Bartlett, is this day dissolved by mutual consent. All persons having claims against the firm are requested to present them for settlement, and all persons indebted to the firm are requested to make immediate payment to the said Edward M. Bartlett, who is duly authorized to settle the business of the firm.

Henry W. Butler
Edward M. Bartlett.

The business will be carried on in future by the subscriber, who will always have on hand, the usual variety in his line.

EDWARD M. BARTLETT.[14]

Joseph Burns

The will of Joseph Burns, of Marple Township, dated 1777 mentions "Some of my Silversmith tools. . ."

Benjamin Campbell

Benjamin Campbell was a silversmith, goldsmith, clock and watch-maker, in Chester County until 1775 when he moved to Hagerstown, Maryland.[15]

William Carpenter

William Carpenter appears as a silversmith in the West Bradford Township tax assessment for 1783.

Benjamin Chandlee

Benjamin Chandlee appears as a silversmith in 1770 and as a goldsmith in 1774 tax assessments for East Nottingham Township.

Abraham Corl

Abraham Corl appears as a silversmith in the East Nantmeal Township tax assessments for 1811, 1812 and 1814. He also worked as a clockmaker and watchmaker in Chester County.[16]

Richard Flower

On March 11, 1785 Isaac Eyre of the Borough of Chester, yeoman sold land in Ridley Township to Richard Flower, of Ridley Township, silversmith.[17]

George Jackson

George Jackson appears as a silversmith in the Kennett Township tax assessment for 1814. His inventory[18] taken on October 16, 1836 included:

Silver Smith's Anvil & Hammers

George Jackson also worked as a clockmaker and watchmaker in Chester County.[19]

Isaac Jackson

Isaac Jackson appears as a silversmith in the 1797 New Garden Township tax assessment.

Curtis G. Jefferis

Curtis G. Jefferis advertised in 1816:

CLOCK AND WATCH MAKING. The subscriber notifies the public general and his friends in particular, that he has commenced the repairing and cleaning of Clocks & Watches in Church street near Mrs. Pearson Inn in West Chester, where he will execute with neatness and despatch, any commands confided to him.

N. B. Also Jewelry Silverware &c. repaired.[20]

CURTIS G. JEFFERIS

In 1817 he advertised:

CLOCK AND WATCH MAKING. THE SUBSCRIBER notifies the public in general, and his friends in particular, that he still continues carrying on the clock and watch making business, in Church street Westchester, and also SILVER-SMITHING, in all its various branches, which will be done in the neatest manner and newest fashion, as he has employed a first rate workman in that business, and intends keeping a constant supply of table, dessert, and tea-spoons on hand. All orders executed with attention and dispatch.

CURTIS G. JEFFERIS [21]

John Le Telier

John Le Telier appears as a farmer and silversmith in the West Marlboro Township tax assessment for 1796. He is listed as having 100 acres, two horses, four cattle, an old stone and log house, old log barn and a shop. Two years later, in the same township, he is listed as a silversmith.

William Malin

The inventory [22] of William Malin, Upper Providence Township, 1696 includes:

To Sundry Silver Smith tooles
To a Silver tankard
To a Childs Cupp
To a papp dish & Spoon
To a Silver Cupp

Samuel Millhouse

Samuel Millhouse appears as a silversmith in the Kennett Township tax assessment for 1783. He also worked as a clockmaker in Chester County. [23]

James Mulraun

James Mulraun appears as "Silver" in the Lower Oxford Township tax assessment for 1805.

John Neel

John Neel appears as a silversmith in the West Marlboro Township tax assessment for 1798.

Amos Nichols

CHESTER Ss. The Juro[rs] for our Lord the King on their assertacons p[r]. S:nt   That Amos Nichols of the County of Chester Silversmith and Andrew Neals all[s] ffreend of the County of New Castle husbandman by force & armes the 2[d] day of January 1699 att or near a certain place called Marcus Creek in the county of Chester aforsd in the Kings highway upon Thomas Howell of Cicell county in Maryland planter an assault did make & him the sd Thomas then & there Evilly handled by cutting off part of his hair whereof they putt him in feare of his life and the sume of One hundred pounds of money numbred from the pson of the said Thomas then & there found upon him (being the goods & chattels of him the sd Thomas did feloneously take & carry away contra[r]y to the Kings peace by crowne & dignity & against the laws in such cases made & provided &c.
bill allowd
Robert varnon
fore man [24]

William D. Parrott

William D. Parrott appears as a silversmith in the East Marlboro Township tax assessment for 1842.

George Peters

George Peters appears as a silversmith in the West Chester tax assessments for 1801 and 1802.

Jas Pyle

Jas Pyle appears as a silversmith in the Chester tax assessment for 1782.

Robert Reilly

Robert Reilly, son of James, silver-smith lived in West Fallowfield Township. The dates are not known. [25]

Joseph H. Seal

Joseph H. Seal appears as a silversmith in the Birmingham Township tax assessment for 1814.

Joseph Shambough

The inventory[26] of Joseph Shambough, of Charlestown Township, taken in 1784 included:

Silver Smith tools

On March 30, 1786 Catharine Shambough, widow of Joseph late of Charlestown township, silversmith, deceased sold a plantation and tract in Charlestown Township to Philip Shambough, of Providence Township, Montgomery county.[27]

Francis W. Smith

Francis W. Smith advertised in 1840:

An Apprentice Wanted. A BOY about 15 or 16 years of age, of good moral habits, will be taken as an apprentice to the Silversmith and Jewelry business by

FRANCIS W. SMITH.[28]

and

FRANCIS W. SMITH, JEWELLER AND SILVERSMITH. THE subscriber being of long experience in the business, respectfully informs his friends and the public in general, that he is prepared to do all

kinds of jobs connected with his business. He will mend and repair all kinds of jewelry, mount guns and canes. He also manufactures jewelry and Surgical instruments of every description, and prepares gold and silver plates for dentists. He will be found at his shop, in Church street, At Mr. Whitehead's, south of Chester County Hotel, or at his residence at the corner of Main and New Streets.

FRANCIS W. SMITH.[29]

. . .N.B Old gold and silver taken in exchange for work. [30]

In 1841 he announces:

REMOVAL. FRANCIS W. SMITH, JEWELLER, has removed his establishment to Gay St., nearly opposite the White Hall Hotel [31]. .

James Smith

James Smith appears as a silversmith in the West Chester tax assessment for 1801.

James Sterrett

James Sterrett appears as a silversmith in the East Nantmeal Township tax assessment for 1785.

John Tanguy

John Tanguy silversmith, in 1831 purchased a farm in Birmingham Township. He lived there until about 1854 when he moved to Westtown Township. John Tanguy died June 15, 1858 in West Goshen Township. Although essentially a farmer while living in the county he also made occasional pieces of silver.

Charles Thacher

Charles Thacher appears as a silversmith in the Tredyffrin Township tax assessment for 1821.

James Way

On March 24, 1780 James Way, silversmith of Thornbury Township was about to return to North Carolina.[32]

Joshua Weaver

Joshua Weaver is listed as a silversmith in Goshen Township in 1783 and 1797 and in West Chester in 1805 and 1806. He was also a conveyor.

In 1827 Joshua Weaver died. His inventory includes: "Lot of tolls (silver smith) (in backshed) $5."[33]

Samuel Williamson

On March 28, 1814 Samuel Baldwin of "Downingstown", tanner, and Mary, his wife sold a tract in Uwchland Township to Samuel Williamson of the city of Philadelphia, Silversmith now of Uwchlan Township, Chester county.[34]

Edward Woolley

Edward Woolley appears as a silver smith in the West Chester tax assessment for 1823 where his name has been crossed out.

Allen Yarnall

Allen Yarnall advertised in 1825:

ALLEN YARNALL CLOCK & WATCH MAKER RESPECTFULLY informs his friends and the public in general, that he has commenced the above business in Sugartown. . .[Willistown Township] where he hopes by strict attention to business to merit a liberal share of public patronage. He has on hand an assortment of Watch Chains, Seals and

Keys, Silver Thimbles, Breast Pins, Finger Rings, &c, &c, which he will dispose of at a very low rate of cash.

N.B. Second handed watches for sale. New Clocks and watches furnished at the shortest notice. Work warranted. [35]

In 1829 he advertised:

Silver Ware and Jewellry, ALLEN YARNALL, HAS opened an establishment, in Gay Street, West Chester, which he hopes will be an accommodation to the citizens generally, and at the same time advantageous to himself, — He has now on hand and offers for sale, Silver Table and Tea Spoons, plated do. silver and plated Sugar Tongs, silver Spectacles, with plain and green glasses, Metallic Pens, ever pointed and plain Pencil Cases, Tailors' and Milliners' silver Thimbles, Tooth Picks, Scissors Hooks and Chains, Finger Guards, Sleeve Buttons, Purse Clasps, Gold Locket Chains, barrel and flat Lockets, Ear and Finger Rings, Hooks for Ladies watches, Breast Pins, Chains, Seals, and Keys of most patterns and qualities. Steel Chains, Seals and Keys, Gilt do.

Eight day Clocks, with Mahogany Cases; eight-day Timepieces, Mantle do (24 hours), Silver cased English watches, new and second handed; Musical Shell Boxes &c.

All of which he will sell at Philadelphia retail prices. The clocks, watches, &c. warranted to perform well for one year free of expense to the purchaser. Clocks delivered at any distance per order. Also, Clocks and Watches repaired, in the neatest manner.

The highest price given for Old Gold or Silver in exchange for work or goods. [36]

Allan Yarnall advertised in 1830:

CLOCK & WATCH REPAIRING. THE subscriber respectfully informs his friends and the public in general, that he still continues to repair Clocks & Watches, at his old stand in Gay-street, West-Chester, nearly opposite Peter Osborne's (Green Tree tavern,) where those that see proper to give him their custom, may be assured, that every exertion will be rendered to accommodate them on the most liberal terms. He has on hand and intends keeping a general assortment of Clocks & Watches, Silverware and Jewelry, &c. Patent Lever and Plain Silver Watches. Eight day Brass Clocks, wooden do. patent. Eight day Timepieces, warranted by Wm. Commins. Mantle do. 24 hours; and a variety of second hand Watches. Silver table and tea spoons, salt spoons, sugar tongs, scissors hooks, purse-clasps, sleeve buttons, tooth picks, coat clasps, barrel lockets, spectacles, with plain and green glasses, taylors' and milliners' silver thimbles, ever pointed pencils, plain and with calendar. Plated table and tea-spoons, sugar tongs, &c. An elegant assortment of gold seals, keys chains, slides and rings, both plain and variegated, plated do. Gold breast pins, set with pearl and garnet, jet pins, filagree and topaz do, a number of fancy broaches, gold ear rings, of different patterns and qualities, gold locket chains, watch hooks, flat and barrel lockets. Also, an assortment of steel chains, seals, keys and rings. Gilt seals, keys and rings, metallic pens, &c.

The above articles will be sold at the lowest Philadelphia prices, and a deduction of five per cent. for cash.

ALLEN YARNALL.

N.B. The highest price given for gold and silver, in exchange for work or goods. [37]

CALL AND SEE FOR YOURSELVES, JUST received from Philadelphia, an assortment of Watches, Silver-Ware, and Jewelry, Ten percent cheaper than ever.

ALLEN YARNALL.[38]

On March 17, 1831 Joshua Gibbons, of the Borough of West Chester, and Martha, his wife sold a log tenement and lot in West Chester to Allen Yarnall of the Borough of West Chester, silversmith.[39]

The inventory[40]of Allen Yarnall taken in West Chester on June 30, 1832 included as well as clock and watchmaking tools:

3 fine gilt watch chains & seals
4 Brass chains various jewelry items
1 Chest of Jewelry & Contents

In Chester county nine of the silversmiths also made clocks and watches. In the eighteenth century there were Benjamin Chandlee and Isaac Jackson. During the nineteenth century, prior to 1850 there were Samuel Millhouse, Abraham Corl, William Baily, George Jackson, Curtis G. Jefferis and George W. Baldwin, Allen Yarnall carried on silversmithing and clock and watchmaking in addition to the jewelry business. Edward M. Bartlett and Henry W. Butler had a jewelry and fancy hardware store in addition to being silversmiths and Francis W. Smith was a silversmith and jeweler.

SILVER and TIN PLATERS

William Apple

In 1832 William Apple, of West Chester, advertised a Copper, Tin and Sheet-Iron Manufactory where he had constantly on hand and for sale,

Copper and Brass Wash Kettles, Tea Kettles, Saucepans, Andirons, Shovels and Tongs, with a general assortment of Tin and Hollow Ware. Tin Spouts and Gutters constantly on hand. Stills of all descriptions made and repaired. Old copper, brass, pewter and lead, taken in exchange.[41]

. . .Also, a handsome assortment of Cannon Coal Stoves.[42]

By 1835 he had added to his stock:

PATENT BAKING OVENS. THE subscriber takes this method of informing his friends, and the public in general, that he has purchased the right of making Hall's portable Patent Baking Ovens for the counties of Chester and Delaware. The body of these Ovens are made of Tin headed on by Iron Cylinders. The whole of the inside of the oven, acting as a reflector, thereby lessening the quantity of fuel necessary in ordinary Baling. Four loaves of bread can be baked, and that too without the disagreeable smell of coal, smoke or dust. Families will find it to their advantage to purchase one of the above articles. They are made of different sizes, and prices in proportion; they can be seen at all times at the store of the subscriber, and on Tuesday's and Friday's [3d and 6th day's] they may be seen in full operation.

COOKING STOVES, common stoves, plain and fancy parlor grates on hand and will be sold low for cash.

Old castings taken in exchange.

WM. APPLE.

Copper and Tin Manufacturer, East end of the Borough of West Chester.[43]

The following year he announced:

. . .The subscriber has also purchased the right of Chester county for making Nott and Co's patent Baking Ovens, they are made somewhat similar to the above, with the addition of a tea kettle boiler and steamer. One gallon of charcoal is sufficient to perform those three additional operations.[44]

In 1841 he advertised:

WHOLESALE & RETAIL Copper, Tin & Sheet-Iron Ware MANU-FACTORY, THE subscriber respectfully informs his friends and the public in general that he still continues to carry on the above business at the old stand in Gay street, nearly opposite the Eagle Hotel, where are constantly kept, all articles in the above line, together with all articles connected with house keeping, such as copper and brass wash kettles, tea kettles, saucepans, &c., andirons, shovel and tongs, knives and forks, table and tea spoons, and irons, &c.

STOVES, of all descriptions for either coal or wood, with an assortment of fancy PARLOUR STOVES. TIN SPOUT and gutters put up at the shortest notice. Buildings covered with tin or copper, and warranted water proof, or no charge. All kinds of copper, lead or iron pipes, furnished and laid on reasonable terms. The PLUMBING Business will also be carried on, in all its various branches.

FURNACES for heating rooms, of the most approved plain, made and fitted up. Cast iron furnace doors finished complete, ready for walling in. All kinds of jobbing done in copper, tin, sheet iron or lead.

BLACKSMITH JOBBING, done as usual.

Old iron copper, brass, pewter and lead taken in exchange.

P.S. From one to fifty cords of oak or hickory wood will be taken in exchange for stoves or tin ware.

WM. APPLE.[45]

In 1847 he mentions:

. . .Among the articles offered are Cooking Stoves, of different patterns, for Coal or wood; plain Wood Stoves, of all sizes; parlour Stoves, Radiators, and air tight stoves; Also, andirons, shovel and tongs, knives and forks, table and tea spoons, sad irons, grid-irons, Copper and Brass wash kettles, preserving kettles, saucepans, iron and tin boilers; JAPANED WARE; milk pans, cream-pots, ice cream cans; all kinds of TIN and SHEET IRON WARE and many other articles too numerous to mention.

N.B. – Copper and Iron Pumps, suitable for wells or cisterns; Also, a quantity of tin house and gutters on hand; Copper chambers for wooden pumps, of the usual sizes, or made to order.[46]

John Barnett

John Barnett appears as a silver plater in the West Chester census for 1842.

Thomas T. Tasker

In 1820 Thomas T. Tasker advertised:

THOMAS T. TASKER,
Tin Plate Worker and Copper Smith, Begs leave to inform the inhabitants of Westchester and its vicinity, that he has commenced business opposite the Spread Eagle tavern, where he intends to carry on the same in all its various branches, and hopes by constant assiduity and punctual attention, to merit the patronage and support of those who may favour him with their commands. Tin or Copper half round Spouting, Valley guttering or Wall pipe with uniform heads of the first quality and finish. Tin and Copper articles repaired in the neatest and most serviceable manner.

Brass, Copper, Pewter, or lead taken in Exchange.[47]

In 1822, at a Sheriff's Sale the following articles of Personal property were sold:

. . .one Milch cow, a variety of Household and Kitchen furniture, consisting of Bureaus, Tables, Chairs, Bedsteads, Candle stand, one Ten plate Stove, Coffee pots, Tea kettles, Gallon, Half gallon, Quart and Pint measures, Sugar scoops, Lanterns, Candle-moulds, Tin cups, Funnels, Candle-boxes, Dripping-pans, Copper Still-head and Worm, Boilers, Tin stoves, Copper pump, Spout heads, Sheet tin, old copper, &c. together with a quantity of Window glass and numerous other articles not inserted here.[48]

Philip Francis Geiss

In 1830 John Reid advertised:

A FI'PENNY-BIT REWARD, AND NO CHARGES. LEFT the service of the subscriber, in June 1829, an Apprentice to the Silver-plating Business — named PHILIP FRANCIS GEISS: about 17 years of age. Whoever will return said Boy to his master, may expect the above reward, precisely—. And all persons are forbidden to harbor or trust said boy—as they would avoid the penalty of the law.

JOHN REID.

Brandywine Township [49]

George Reid

George Reid appears as a silver plater in the West Caln Township tax assessment for 1828. On April 3, 1832 George Reid, of Brandywine Township, silver plater, and Esther his wife sold land to William Stanley of Brandywine Township.[50]

James Reid

James Reid appears as a silver plater in the Brandywine Township tax assessment for 1828. On March 31, 1828 John Butler, of Brandywine Township, turner, and his wife, Jane sold to James Reed of Brandywine Township, silver plater land in Brandywine Township.[51] On September 28, 1836 James Reid of Brandywine Township, silver plater, and wife Mary sold land in Brandywine Township to John Forbes, farmer.[52]

John Reid

On March 31, 1827 Isaac Williams and John Williams sold land in Brandywine Township, to John Reid, of Brandywine Township, silver plater.[53] John Reid appears in 1827 as a silver plater in the West Caln Township tax assessment. On April 1, 1828 James Mendenhall, of Brandywine Township, sold land to John Reid, silver plater, of Brandywine Township, land in Brandywine Township.[54] In 1830 John Reid advertised:

> A FI'PENNY-BIT REWARD, AND NO CHARGES. LEFT the service of the subscriber, in June, 1829, an Apprentice to the Silver-plating Business--named PHILIP FRANCIS GEISS: about 17 years of age. Whoever will return said Boy to his master, may expect the above reward, precissly--. And all persons are forbiden to harbor or trust said boy--as they would avoid the penalty of the law.
> JOHN REID.
> Brandywine township[55]

On April 2, 1834 John Reid, of Brandywine Township, silver plater, and Rebecca his wife sold land in Brandywine Township to Mary Trago, of Brandywine Township.[56]

William Reid

William Reid appears as a silver plater in the West Caln Township tax assessment for 1828. In 1829 he advertised:

> Plated Saddlery. WILLIAM REID, SILVER-PLATER, HAS opened an establishment in Gay-st. West-Chester, opposite to Titus Bennett's Confectionary, which he hopes will be an accommodation to Saddlers and Harness-Makers, and at the same time a little advantage to himself. He keeps on hand, besides plated Saddlery, Saddle-trees, cotton and worsted Web, Saddler's Silk, Curry combs, &c. at Philadelphia prices, which he will sell at prices that cannot fail to please, for ready cash.
> N.B. Bridle-bit, Stirrup and Coach-harness Plating carried on in all its various branches. [57]

In 1833 he advertised:

> WILLIAM REID, Manufacturer of PLATED SADDLERY, North-west corner of Church, and Chestnut streets— TAKES this method of informing his friends and the public, that he continues to carry on the above business in all its branches; keeping constantly on hand a good assortment of bridle bitts, stirrup irons, spurs, buckles of all sizes and qualities, plated, japan'd and tin'd harness mountings, wheel hands, plated ornaments, saddle trees, wood hammers, New-England and city dress'd hog skins, whip stocks, halter chains, linen, cotton and worsted webbs, saddler's silk, and all kinds of articles generally used by saddlers and coach-makers. All kinds of coach iron work, Door-knobs, bell-pulls, bridle bitts, stirrups, &c. plated with Brass or Silver at the shortest notice, and on the most reasonable terms for cash. [58]

In 1834 he advertised for sale:

> . . .and has on hand and for sale, all kinds of bridle bits, stirrup irons, stump, dashes and handles, plated and japan'd, coach, gig and dearborne mountings, saddle trees, girth and straining webb, plated moulding for gigs and saddlers, all kinds of mountings for bridles, saddler's

silk, plated and metal knobs, stump joints, buckles of all sizes and descriptions, bright and black halter chains, saddler's tacks of the best quality and of all sizes.

N B All kinds of Coach work plated at the shortest notice and on the most reasonable terms. All orders from a distance attended to.[59]

William Reid appears as a silver plater in the West Chester tax assessment for 1835. That year he advertised:

Removal. WILLIAM REID Silver Plater & manufacture of plated Saddlery RESPECTFULLY informs his friends and the public that he still carries on the above business, in all its various branches, in Gay St a few rods West of the Cross Keys.[60]

George Harris Rudd

"George Harris Rudd, aged Fourteen Years & Eight days (whose Father is dead) with the Coment of his mother now Sally Burgess of Chester County expressed in an instrument of writing to the Indenture annexed, & also with the approbation of his uncle William Lewis Sonntag of the city of Philadia bound apprentice to William Barry of the Said city Silver Plater for Six Years Eleven months and twenty one days to learn the art, trade & mistery of a Silver Plater.[61] ."

TIN

The following men are listed in the public records.

Baldwin, John (tin plate worker)	West Caln Twp.	1753-1766
	East Caln Twp.	1762
	East Caln Twp.	1782-1784
Busser, Henry (tin plate mfg.)	Sadsbury Twp.	1842
Busser, Jacob M. (tin plate mfg.)	Sadsbury Twp.	1842
Christy, Charles (tin plate worker)	East Nottingham Twp.	1827
Cristy, John (tinner)	Lower Oxford Twp.	1842
Collier, William S. (tinner)	East Marlboro Twp.	1842
Hartman, Daniel (tinner)	West Vincent Twp.	1842-1843
Johnson, Joshua (tin plate worker)	Darby Twp.	1712
Kendle, William P. (tinman)	Kennett Twp.	1842
Lent, John (tin mfg. & sheet iron)	West Chester	1842
Rattew John (tin plate worker)	West Chester	1802
	Goshen Twp.	1809
Rettew, John, Jr. (tinman)		1808
Romans, Moses (tin plate worker)	West Bradford Twp.	1842
Steel, Isaac P. (tin & stove merchant)	New London Twp.	1849
Stephens, Samuel R. (tinman)	Kennett Twp.	1842
Tatherard, William (tinman)	Honeybrook Twp.	1842
Taylor, Thomas (tin & copper plate)	West Chester	1821
Watson, Henry (tin plate worker)	West Chester	1823
Wickersham, J. Jefferis (tin plate)	West Chester	1842
Wollett, William (tinman)	Sadsbury Twp.	1812

WHITESMITH

A whitesmith is defined by the Oxford English Dictionary [ed. 1933] as "a. A worker in white iron; a tinsmith. b. One who polishes or finishes metal goods, as distinguished from one who forges them; also more widely, a worker in metals."

The following men are listed in the public records.

Dunmar, Matthew	Coventry Twp.	1816
	East Nantmeal Twp.	1817
Granger, John	Brandywine Twp.	1842
Pilkington, Edward	Chichester Twp.	1788
Pilkerton, Jos.	Middletown Twp.	1779
Pilkerton, Thomas	Middletown Twp.	1779-1782
Sutlar, Samuel	West Caln Twp.	1817
Taylor, John	Charlestown Twp.	1814
Winter, George	Vincent Twp.	1825

Parkesburg house, Parkesburg
Built ca. 1825

Fire back made at the Reading Furnace in Warwick township. 23" by 24".

Mr. and Mrs. Samuel W. Morris collection

Fire back dated 1734. It was found in the Sharpless house in Birmingham township. 26" by 20".

Chester County Historical Society collection

Franklin stove signed "MORDECAI PEIRSOL." The stove was made at Rebecca Furnace in West Nantmeal township, ca. 1787-1789.
Chester County Historical Society collection

st iron cook stove marked "COOKS FAVOURITE" and "CYRUS
MBORN CHESTER COUNTY." Early nineteenth century.
Salem, Inc.

Foot scraper. Height 18 1/4",
width 13 1/2".
Chester County Historical Society collection.

Weathervane of the Pris[
erected in West Chester
1838.
Chester County Historical Society col[

Weathervane from the First
West Chester Fire Company
incorporated in 1799.
Chester County Historical Society collection.

Weathervane on the mill owned by William Penn, Samuel Carpenter and Caleb Pusey.

Historical Society of Pennsylvania collection.

Rain spout made by William Apple. It was on his store at the southeast corner of Gay and Walnut Streets in West Chester.

Chester County Historical Society collection.

Squirrel cage. Height 24", width 36", depth 11".

Chester County Historical Society collection.

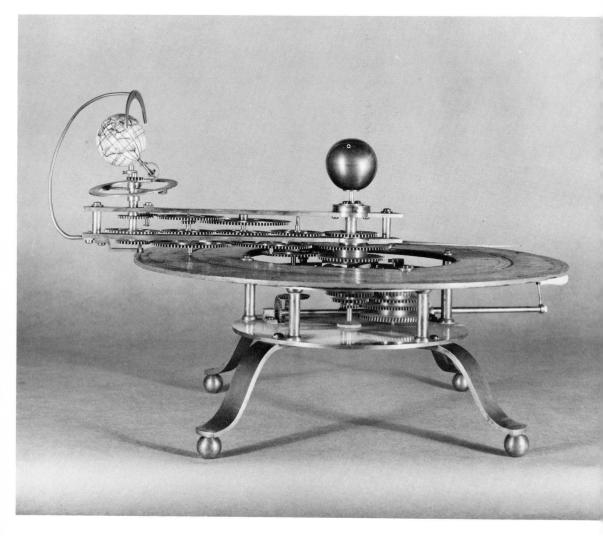

Brass orrery "Made by A. Willand, Jr. Boston for the West Chester Academy."

Chester County Historical Society collection.

Brass surveyor's compass. Made by Ellis and Isaac Chandlee. Working
in East Nottingham Township, ca. 1795.

Chester County Historical Society collection.

Wood surveyor's compass made by Abraham Darlington (b. 1723–
d. 1799).

Chester County Historical Society collection.

[1] *Village Record,* (West Chester, Pa.), May 18, 1841.

[2] *American Republican,* (West Chester, Pa.), Aug. 30, 1814.

[3] *Anti-Masonic Register,* (West Chester, Pa.), July 11, 1832.

[4] *Chester County Deed Book,* N-4, p. 316.

[5] Margaret B. Schiffer, *Furniture and Its Makers of Chester County, Pennsylvania,* (Phila., Pa.), 1966, p. 26.

[6] *American Republican,* (West Chester, Pa.), Sept. 9, 1834.

[7] *Village Record,* (West Chester, Pa.), Oct. 29, 1834.

[8] Ibid., Nov. 25, 1835.

[9] Ibid., Aug. 9, 1836.

[10] *American Republican,* (West Chester, Pa.), March 26, 1839.

[11] Ibid., May 19, 1840.

[12] *American Republican,* (West Chester, Pa.), April 1, 1834.

[13] Ibid., May 20, 1834.

[14] Ibid., Sept. 9, 1834.

[15] Ms. No. 76540, *Chester County Historical Society,* (West Chester, Pa.).

[16] Margaret B. Schiffer, *Furniture and Its Makers of Chester County, Pennsylvania,* (Phila., Pa., 1966), p. 58.

[17] *Chester County Deed Book Z,* p. 103.

[18] Arthur E. James, *Chester County Clocks and Their Makers,* (West Chester, Pa., 1947), p. 151.

[19] Margaret B. Schiffer, *Furniture and Its Makers of Chester County, Pennsylvania,* (Phila., Pa., 1966), p. 126.

[20] *Chester & Delaware Federalist,* (West Chester, Pa.), April 17, 1816.

[21] Ibid., June 4, 1817.

[22] *Philadelphia Estate Papers,* p. 1527.

[23] Margaret B. Schiffer, *Furniture and Its Makers of Chester County, Pennsylvania,* (Phila., Pa., 1966), p. 161

[24] *Chester County Historical Society,* (West Chester, Pa.), Ms. Industries Silversmithing.

[25] *Ms. Industries Silversmith,* Chester County Historical Society, (West Chester, Pa.).

[26] *Chester County Inventories No. 3624.*

[27] *Chester County Deed Book D-2,* p. 17

[28] *Register & Examiner* (West Chester, Pa.), Nov. 17, 1840.

[29] Ibid., Sep. 1, 1840.

[30] *American Republican,* (West Chester, Pa.), Sep. 1, 1840.

[31] *Register & Examiner,* (West Chester, Pa.), Aug. 31, 1841.

[32]*Chester County Letters of Attorney Book A*, p. 49.

[33]*Chester County Inventories No. 8090.*

[34]*Chester County Deed Book K-3*, p. 271.

[35]*Village Record*, (West Chester, Pa.), May 25, 1825.

[36]*American Republican*, (West Chester, Pa.), June 2, 1829.

[37]*Village Record*, (West Chester, Pa.), May 12, 1830.

[38]Ibid., Dec. 8, 1830.

[39]*Chester County Deed Book D-4*, p. 403.

[40]*Chester County Inventories No. 8837.*

[41]*Chester County Democrat*, (West Chester, Pa.), Aug. 21, 1832.

[42]*Village Record*, (West Chester, Pa.), Nov. 7, 1832.

[43]Ibid., March 18, 1835.

[44]Ibid., Sept. 28, 1836.

[45]Ibid., Sept. 28, 28

[46]*American Republican*, (West Chester, Pa.), May 8, 1849.

[47]*Village Record*, (West Chester, Pa.), Aug. 9, 1820.

[48]Ibid., April 23, 1823.

[49]*Village Record*, (West Chester, Pa.), July 28, 1830.

[50]*Chester County Deed Book F-4*, p. 62.

[51]*Chester County Deed Book G-4*, p. 373.

[52]*Chester County Deed Book M-4*, p. 685.

[53]*Chester County Deed Book Z-3*, p. 414

[54]*Chester County Deed Book A-4*, p. 435.

[55]*Village Record*, (West Chester, Pa.), July 28, 1830.

[56]*Chester County Deed Book H-4*, p. 379.

[57]*Village Record*, (West Chester, Pa.), May 18, 1841.

[58]*American Republican*, (West Chester, Pa.), Aug. 30, 1814.

[59]*Anti-Masonic Register*, (West Chester, Pa.), July 11, 1832.

[60]*Chester County Deed Book*, N-4, p. 316.

[61]*Apprenticeship Papers Archives*, City Hall, (Phila., Pa.).

Needlework

Dresden-type samplers were embroidered during the latter half of the eighteenth century. A Dresden sampler was worked on a linen or cotton ground. Sections of the ground were cut out and filled in with needlemade lace, using the buttonhole or hollie point stitch. Hollie point is a twisted buttonhole stitch.

1721 sampler of Ann Marsh. Embroidered in silk on linen using cross, satin, long and short, eyelet, stem and french knot stitches. 14 1/2" by 11 1/2".
George N. Highley Estate

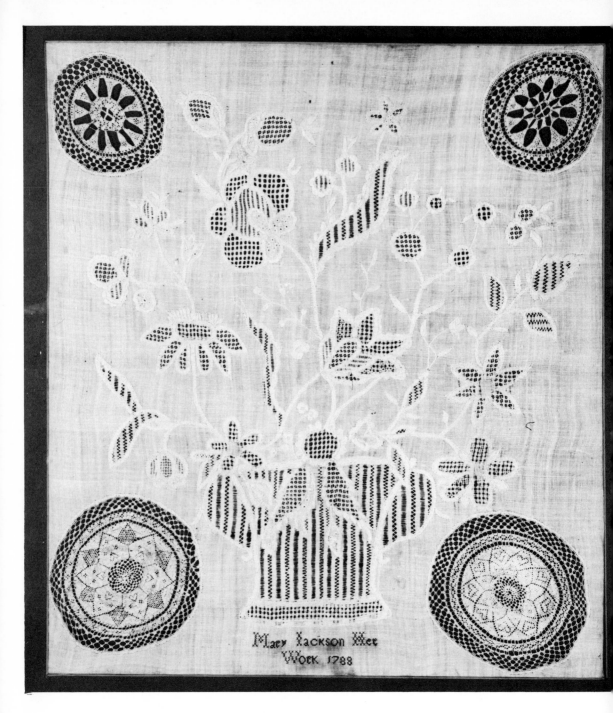

1788 Dresden sampler of Mary Jackson.
Chester County Historical Society collection.

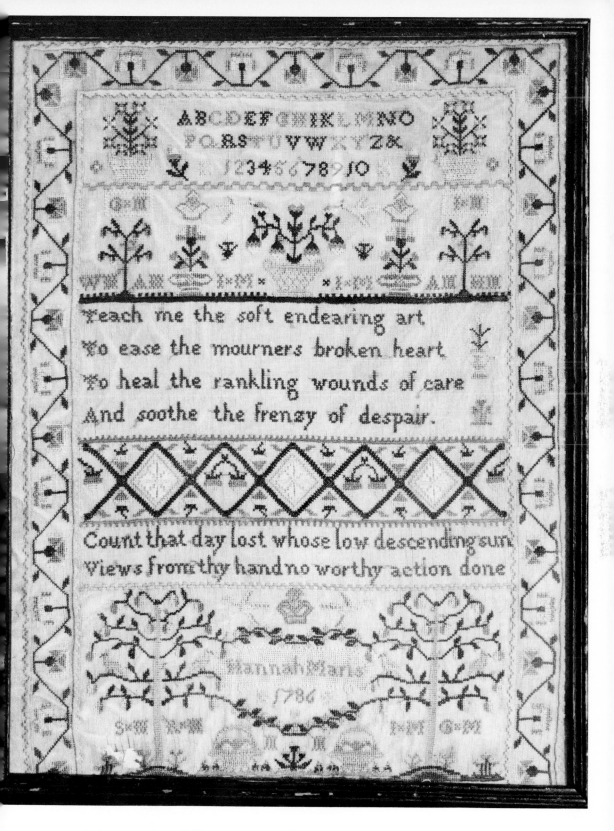

1786 sampler of Hannah Maris. Worked in silk on linen using cross, satin and petit point stitches. 17″ by 13″.

Mrs. Herbert F. Schiffer collection.

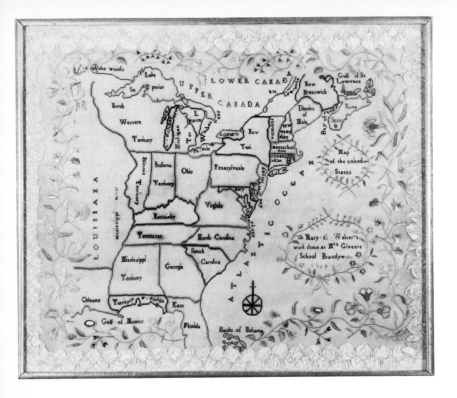

1813 "Map of the United States" by Mary H. Walter worked at Mrs. Given's School, Brandywine. Embroidered in silk on linen using petit point, satin, long and short, stem and chain stitches. Around the border is a quilled ribbon. 24″ by 20″.
Chester County Historical Society collection.

1823 sampler made by Ann H. Vodges of Wilistown township, at fifteen years of age. Embroidered in silk on linen using cross, satin and long stitches. 25″ by 23″:
Mr. and Mrs. Theodore Kapnek collection.

Sampler worked by Mary H. Garrett (born 1805, died 1831) of Willis-
town township. Embroidered in silk on linen using satin, chain, cross,
out line and bullion knot stitches. There is a quilled ribbon border.
27″ by 21 1/2″.

Mr. and Mrs. Theodore Kapnek collection.

1842 sampler by Mary Ann Baily. Embroidered in wool on linen
using cross, satin, and stem stitches. There is a green ribbon border
on four sides and a rosette in each corner. 21″ by 25 1/2″.

Mrs. Herbert F. Schiffer collection.

1824 sampler marked "Mary Graves was born 2nd mo the 28th 1789 and done this work with Hannah G. Carpenter in the Year of our Lord 1824." Embroidered in silk on linen using cross, satin and petit point stitches. 32" by 30".

Mrs. Herbert F. Schiffer collection.

1833 sampler by Phebe M. Halls. Hannah and Jane Pyle were her teachers. Embroidered in silk using satin and cross stitches. There is a quilled ribbon border with two rosettes. 24" by 22 1/2".
Chester County Historical Society collection

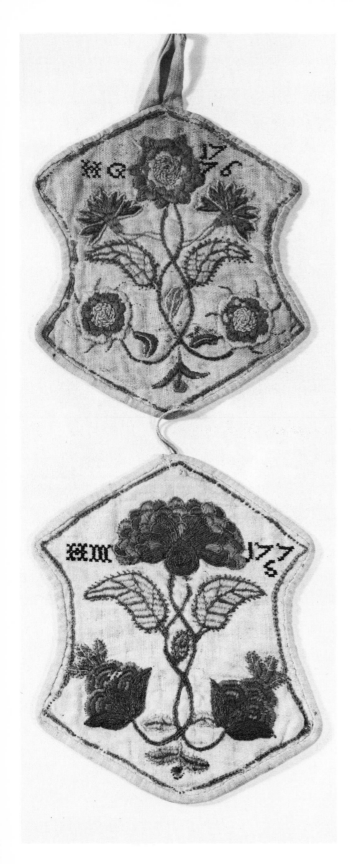

Pot holders initialed and dated "H M 1775". Embroidered in crewel using satin, stem, feather, bullion knot and chain stiches. Height 6 1/2", width 4 1/2" to 5 1/2".

Mrs. Joseph Russell collection

Woman's crewel pocket initialed "S B". Embroidered in wool, using cross, chain and roumanian stitches. 15″ by 12 1/2″.

Mrs. Herbert F. Schiffer collection.

1791 crewel work picture initialed "E G". Embroidered in wool and using stem, satin, bullion, knot, cross and long and short stitches. 33 1/2″ by 28″.

Mrs. Herbert F. Schiffer collection.

1774 Silk embroidered picture of Jane Hoopes. Worked in silk on silk using outline, satin, bullion knot and fishbone stitches. 9 1/2" by 8".

Mrs. Herbert F. Schiffer collection.

1791 Silk embroidered picture of Hannah Maris. Worked in silk on silk using long and short, outline and satin stitches. 14" by 11 1/2".

Mrs. Herbert F. Schiffer collection.

Picture worked by Ann Marsh. Embroidered in silk and metallic threads, on satin, using french knot and long and short stitches. 7 1/2" by 8 1/2".

Chester County Society Historical collection.

Silk embroidered pocketbook made for George Brinton (born 1756, died 1846). Worked using chain, buttonhole, satin, roumanian, outline and cross stitches. 8″ by 5″.
Chester County Historical Society collection.

Cushion worked by Ann Marsh who died in Chester County in 1796. Embroidered in silk and wool on canvas, using cross and petit point stitches. 22″ by 17 1/2″.
Chester County Historical Society collection

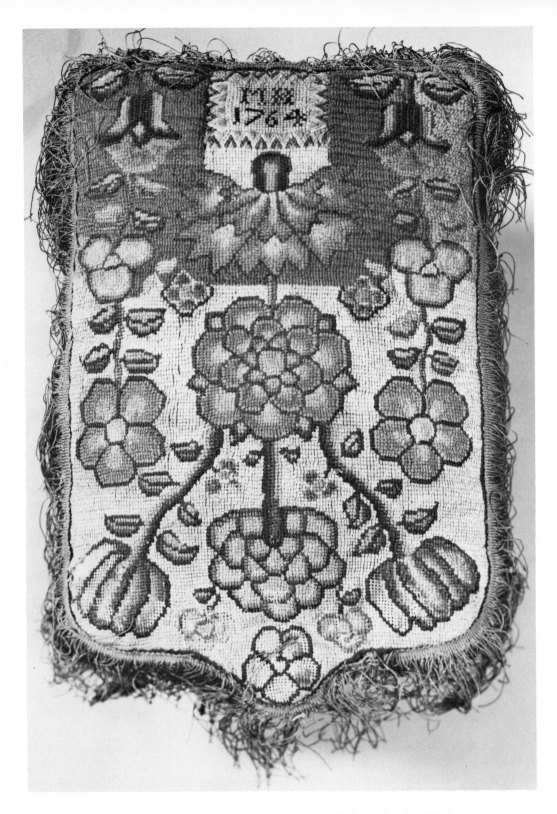

Pincushion initialed and dated "M H 1764" for Martha Hickman. Worked in wool, on canvas, using cross and tent stitches. 10″ by 6 1/2″.
Chester County Historical Society collection.

Pincushion initialed "H P 1746" for Hannah Pennock. Embroidered in cross and rococco stitches. 3"

Mrs. Herbert F. Schiffer collection.

t cover initialed and dated
P 1763" for Lydia Painter.
broidered in Florentine
h, in wool, on a canvas
nd. 20" by 19".

er County Historical Society collection.

Pincushion initialed "S P 1763". Embroidered in Florentine and cross stitches on canvas.
Mrs. Herbert F. Schiffer collection.

Pocket-books worked in Florentine stitch.
Chester County Historical Society.

Wall pocket to hold an alma-
nac. Embroidered in Florentine stitch. 7 1/4" by 8 1/2".

Chester County Historical Society collection.

Women's Pockets worked in Florentine stitch. Pockets were worn under the outer skirt to hold the articles that a woman would need.
Height 13 1/4", width 5 3/4" to 10".

Chester County Historical Society collection.

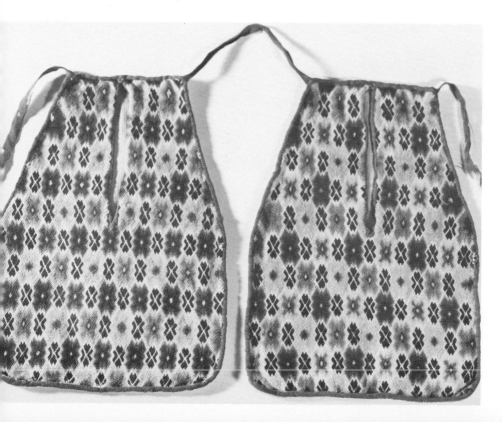

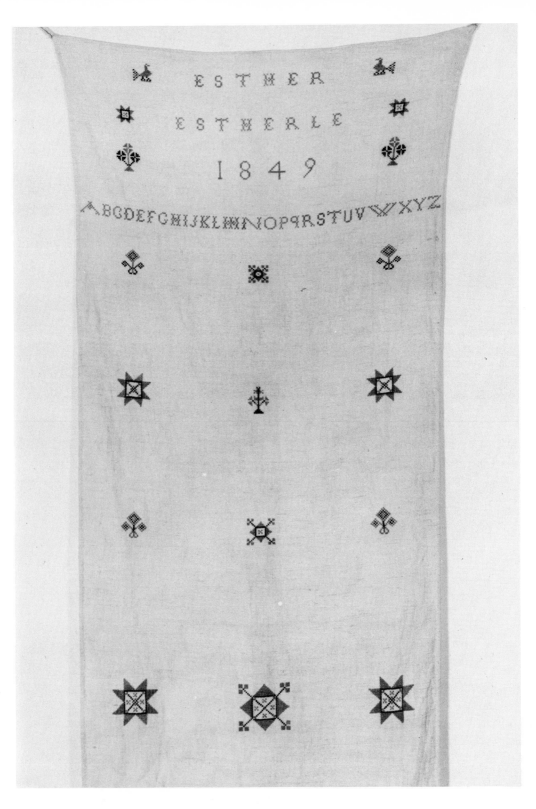

1849 show towel of Esther Estherle. Embroidered in cotton, on linen, using cross stitch. 52″ by 14″.

Chester County Historical Society collection.

88   Mourning Picture of
garetta Bull in memory of
    grandmother Margaretta
obs.   Embroidered on silk
ilk.   21 3/4" by 22 3/4".
er County Historical Society collection.

Tumpunto Bureau cover dated 1831.
26 1/2" by 42 1/2".
Chester County Historical Society collection.

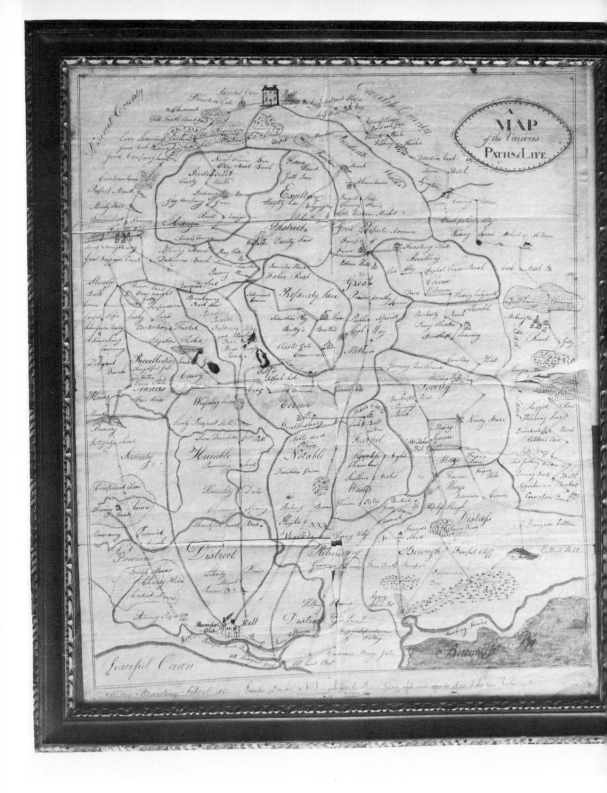

"A Map of the Various Paths of Life" in water color. "Weston Boarding School 1800 Presented 4th Mo. 1806 to R. P. — with hope, she will excuse its many defects, nor ever <u>expose</u> the <u>Name</u> of the poor Performer." 17 1/2″ by 15″.

Mrs. Herbert F. Schiffer collection.

WESTTOWN SCHOOL

Westtown Boarding School, in Westtown Township, opened on May 6, 1799 with twelve or thirteen students. The school was under the supervision of the Philadelphia Yearly Meeting of the Society of Friends. It was for the children of Friends only, the school's aim being to give the boys and girls a guarded religious education under teachers who were religious men and women dedicated to the principles of the Society of Friends. On 4th Month, 11, 1799 a circular was issued: "INFORMATION For Parents and others inclining to send Children for Education to the Friend's boarding school at West-Town" announcing the opening of the school, how to apply, the cost of tuition, listing the clothing necessary for both boys and girls and mentioning: "The girls are also to bring with them a pair of Scissors, Thread-case, Thimble, Work-bag and some plain sewing or knitting to begin with."

The girls study practically the same subjects as the boys. The chief difference is that sewing is emphasized, and that consequently there is time for only elementary mathematics. Two weeks in six are spent in the sewing school, from which the girls go to reading and writing classes as usual, but during the rest of the time they are busy with the needle. Plain sewing comes first, and darning as well. A piece twelve by eight inches must be so perfectly darned that the mending can scarcely be distinguished from the original material. This examination passed, the students undertake the complex embroidery of spectacle cases, globes representing the earth, and samplers with beautifully stitched designs bordering alphabets and moral sentiments, usually in poetry. Some of the more proficient are allowed to stitch views of the School, to be framed and exhibited as pictures, but this, as well as the making of elaborate samplers, is frowned on by the Committee as "Superfluous," and to be discouraged.

Classes are attended regularly, and the time was allowed for learning plain sewing and darning; the more expert graduated to the working of embroidery. Delicate and intricate masterpieces of fancy-work served to hold the interest of the girls during the time of recreation which, in a later age, would be given over to exercise. [1]

Examples of a variety of different types of needlework worked by the students are known: samplers with alphabets, darning samplers, samplers with geometric designs, samplers with pious verses, terrestrial

193

and celestial silk globes and a few pictures of the red brick school building.

The "mending" or "darning" sampler was the first sampler to be made by the students. There were five or seven different stitches worked onto the white or sometimes gray-blue linen ground. It was necessary to work pattern darning samplers on a material, such as linen or muslin, that had threads even enough to be counted. The darning stitches would be worked in a contrasting color to the ground. In this way girls were taught a useful skill, that of mending fabrics invisibly. The spelling "Weston" for "Westtown" School is quite common.

In the early nineteenth century the students made terrestrial and celestial silk globes. There is little needlework on the globes. The longitude and latitude lines are couched down and the borders of countries are worked in the outline stitch. The ships, animals, people and names of countries and oceans are painted in black on the ground. Sometimes the globes were set into small stands made especially for them.

A girl wrote home in reference to the embroidered globes:

I expect to have a good deal of trouble in making them, yet I hope that they will recompense me for all my trouble, for they will certainly be a curiosity to you and of considerable use in instructing my brothers and sisters, and to strengthen my own memory, respecting the supposed shape of our earth, and the manner in which it moves (or is moved) on its axis, or the line drawn through it, round which it revolves every 24 hours. [2]

[1]Helen G. Holz, *Westtown Through the Years 1799-1942,* (Westtown, Pa.), 1942, p. 56.

[2]Watson, W. and Sarah B. Dewees, *History of Westtown Boarding School 1799-1899,* (Phila, Pa.), p. 56.

Westtown old school building.

Written on the back of the frame: "Supposed to have been the work
of Deborah Philips in 1804." Embroidered in silk, on fine linen, using
stem, satin, cross and chain stitches. The colors used are red, green,
tan, yellow, black and white. 14 1/2″ by 9 1/2″.

Westtown School collection.

195

Water color of Westtown School marked "J. COLLINS 1892".
15 3/4″ by 11 1/4″.
Mrs. Herbert F. Schiffer collection.

Sampler of Sarah N. Barton showing Westtown School Building. Embroidered in silk, on linen in cross stitch. The colors used are brown, green, tan, black and white. 11 1/2″ by 7″.
Westtown School collection

1800 Sampler of Elizabeth Humphreys, worked at Westtown School. Embroidered in silk, on linen, in cross stitch. The colors used are red, green, tan, black and white. 14 1/2″ by 12 1/2″.
Westtown School collection.

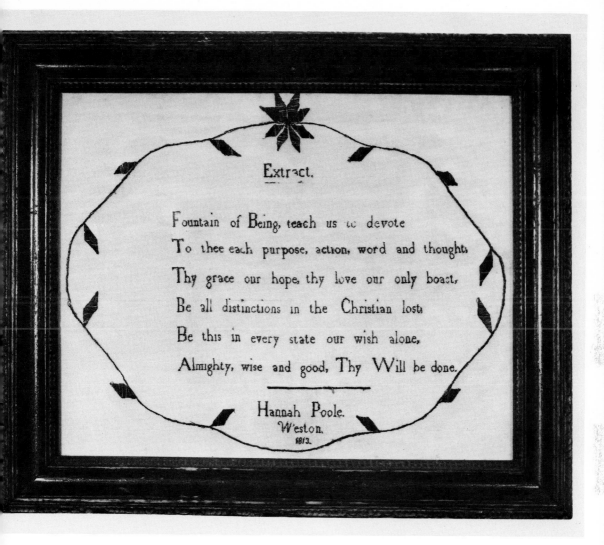

Extract.

Fountain of Being, teach us to devote
To thee each purpose, action, word and thought;
Thy grace our hope, thy love our only boast,
Be all distinctions in the Christian lost;
Be this in every state our wish alone,
Almighty, wise and good, Thy Will be done.

Hannah Poole.
Weston.
1813.

1813 darning sampler of Hannah Poole, worked at Westtown School. Embroidered in white on a gray-green linen, using cross stitch. 9 1/2″ by 9 1/2″.

Mrs. Herbert F. Schiffer collection.

1813 darning sampler of Hannah Poole, worked at the Westtown
School. Embroidered in white on a gray-green linen, using cross stitch.
16″ by 13 1/2″.

Mrs. Herbert F. Schiffer collection.

Terrestial and Celestial silk globes worked by Mary Dickinson who
entered Westtown School in 1814. Height 4 1/2″.

Chester County Historical Society collection.

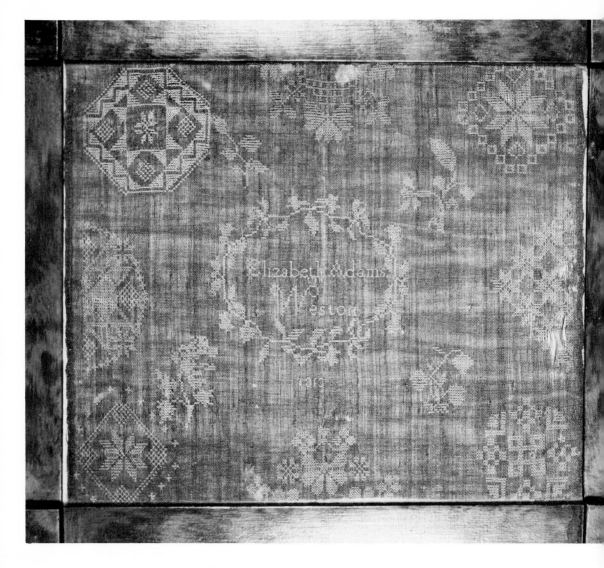

1813 sampler of Elizabeth Adams worked at the Westtown School.
Embroidered in white on a gray-green linen, using cross stitch. 16″
by 13 1/2″.

Mrs. Herbert F. Schiffer collection.

1837 sampler marked "R B M July 1837 Weston Boarding School House". Embroidered on linen using cross and tent stitches. The colors used are brown, tan, red, blue, green, pink, black, yellow, gray, pink, purple, lavender and white. 18″ by 18″.

Mrs. Herbert F. Schiffer collection.

Walnut tilt top candlestand. Height 27″, diameter of top 18″.
Mrs. Herbert F. Schiffer collection

Queen Anne style candlestands and tea tables with snake feet, cabriole legs, depressed ball or bulbous post turnings, birdcage and dish tops were popular for a long period. A Chester County cabinet-maker in the Downingtown area in the second half of the eighteenth century has here added a distinctly local touch—a circular birdcage with either three or four posts. The tables were made of walnut.

Paintings

FOLK ART

1789 Fraktur (Vorschrift) attributed to Jacob Oberholtzer. Made for Johannes Miller in Vincent Township.

Courtesy, the Henry Francis du Pont Winterthur Museum

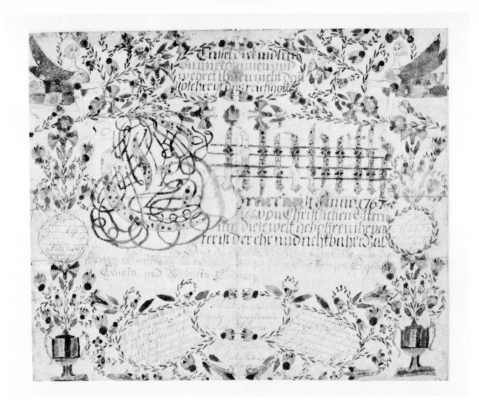

Fraktur Taufschein ca. 1790-1830. 13″ by 15 15/16″.
Courtesy, the Henry Francis du Pont Winterthur Museum

1809 Fraktur Songbook attributed to Jacob Oberholtzer. Made for
George Miller in Chester County. 4″ by 6 9/16″.
Courtesy, the Henry Francis du Pont Winterthur Museum

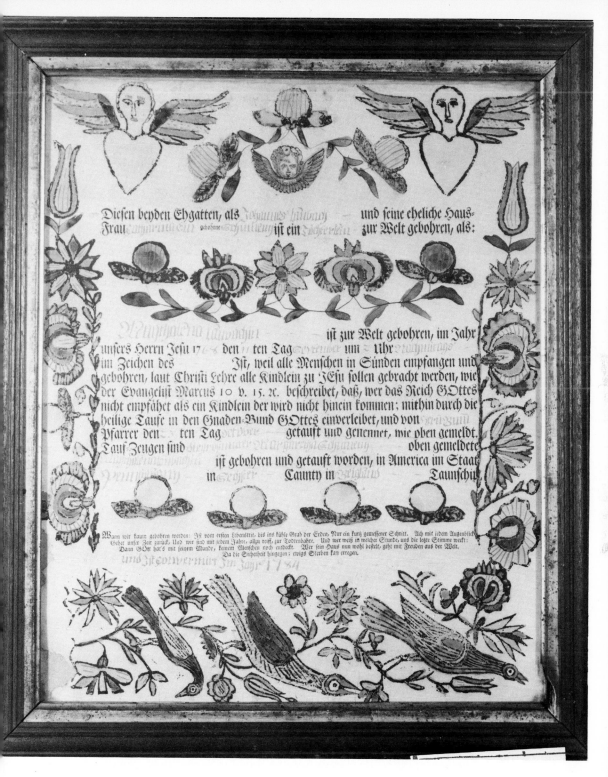

1784 Taufschein made for Magthalena Lubach of Pikeland Township.
17″ by 14″.

Chester County Historical Society collection

1789 Fraktur (Sing-Bild) attributed to Jacob Oberholtzer. Made for Maria Millerin in Vincent Township.

Courtesy, the Henry Francis du Pont Winterthur Museum

Painting on tin by Jane A. Pratt (1837-1927), of West Chester. 11 1/2″ by 9″.

Chester County Historical Society collection.

Cyphering book of "David Horne 5th Feb[ry] 1797". 11 1/2″ by 8″.
Chester County Historical Society collection.

Theorem on velvet. 16 1/2″ by 15 3/4″.
Chester County Historical Society collection.

Water color of the Humphrey Marshall house, in West Bradford Township. Signed "PS". Ca. 1870. 26″ by 20″.

Chester County Historical Society collection

Primitive Hall.
Built in 1738, by Joseph Pennock.
West Marlborough, Chester County.

1842 or 1843 drawing of Primitive Hall in East Marlboro Township.
This is a center square in an authograph patch work quilt.
Chester County Historical Society collection

Water color pictures of houses and outbuildings in East Whiteland Township.

Chester County Historical Society collection.

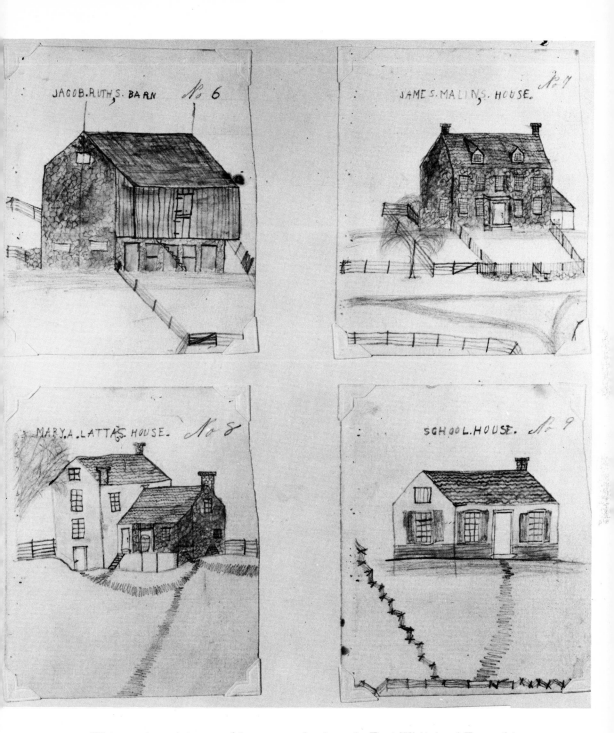

Water color pictures of houses and a barn in East Whiteland Township.
Chester County Historical Society collection.

Water color signed "John 1828 Worth". 18″ by 13″.
Chester County Historical Society collection.

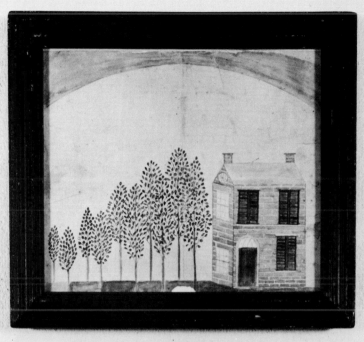

Water color pictures. Top: Painted by Rachel Ann Worth 9 3/4″ by 5 1/2″. Bottom: "House built for Jack by Beckley." The date stone on the house is marked "1825 9 mo 6". 11″ by 9 1/2″.

Chester County Historical Society collection.

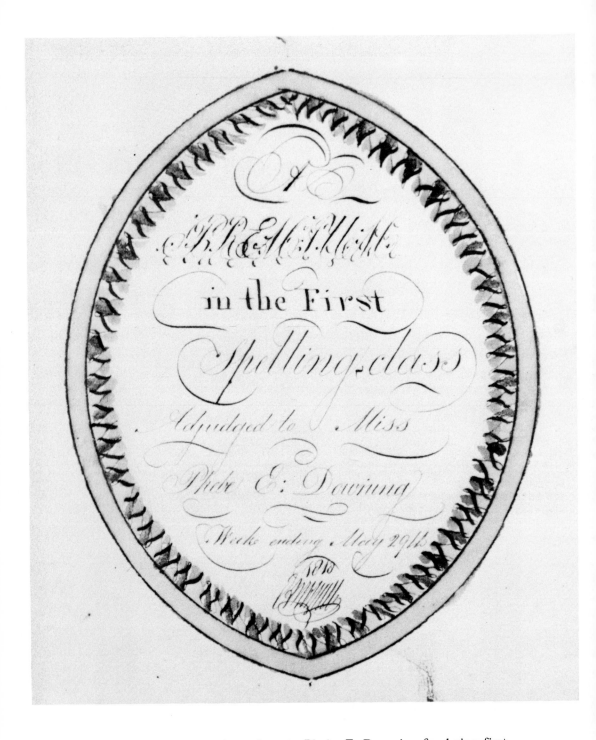

1818 Water color premium given to Phebe E. Downing for being first in spelling class. 6″ by 7″.

Mrs. Herbert F. Schiffer collection.

Nineteenth century Eldridge Family Record. Water color. The border
is quilled ribbon. 15″ by 13″.

Chester County Historical Society collection.

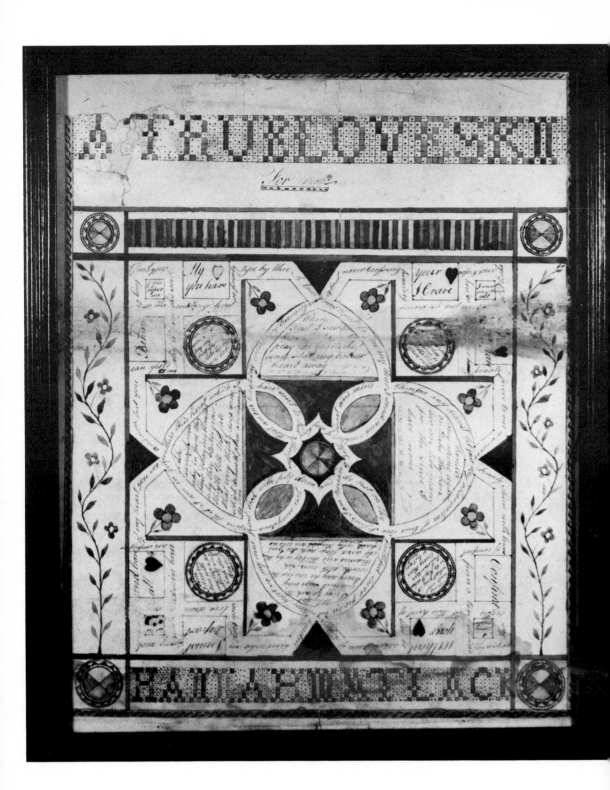

Water color valentine. "A TRUE LOVERS KNOT" for Hannah Matlack,
Goshen Township, born 1814, died 1846. 17 1/2″ by 14 1/2″.
Chester County Historical Society collection.

Water color valentine. 14″ by 14″.
Chester County Historical Society collection.

Water color marked "Mereb Taylors Picture Wrote the 3mo the 13th 1799". 14 1/2″ by 9 1/2″.

Chester County Historical Society collection.

Hymn books attributed to Jacob Oberholtzer. Top: Book of Anna Holdrmanin, Pikeland Township. 1791. 3 3/4″ by 6 1/2″. Bottom: Book of Catarina Carlin, Vincent Township, 1788. 3 3/4″ by 6 1/2″. *Chester County Historical Society collection.*

Water color marked "Elizabeth Downing. Downings Town Chester County y^e 1st Mo y^e 27 1780". 14 1/2″ by 10 1/2″. *Miss Sarah Thomas collection.*

Fraktur: Birth and Baptismal Certificate printed ca. 1829-1835 by Gustav S. Peters in Harrisburg. Completed form has Vincent Township on it. 15 15/16″ by 12 15/16″.

Courtesy, the Henry Francis du Pont Winterthur Museum

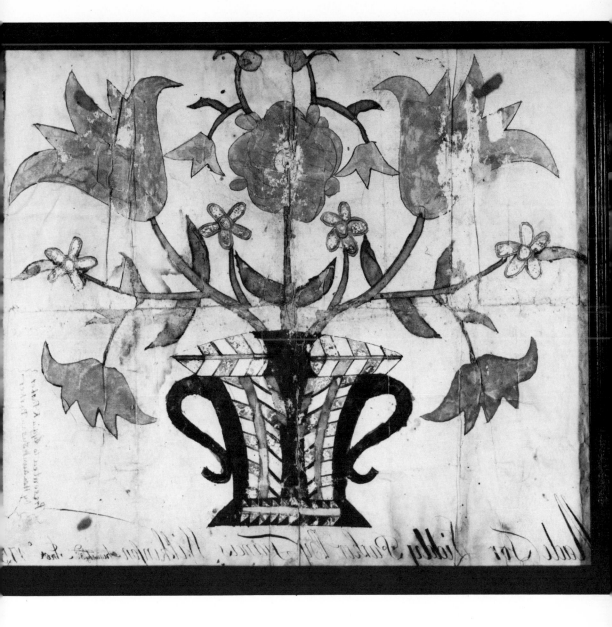

Water color marked "Made for Liddy Parker by Francis Wilkinson August y 3d Anno 1757". Francis Wilkinson was born December 15, 1741 in Bradford Township. His family immigrated from County Antrim, Ireland in 1737. 15 1/2″ by 14″.

Chester County Historical Society collection.

Nineteenth century cut out made by Sarah R. Bowman, West Chester.
5″ by 3″.
Chester County Historical Society collection.

Charcoal on sandpaper picture of Marshallton Friends Meeting, in
West Bradford Township, built in 1765.
Mrs. Robert K. Long collection.

Water color of the Beehive in Westtown Township by Hettie Strode
Brinton (1833-1922). 15 1/2″ by 11 1/2″.
Chester County Historical Society collection.

Theorem by Henrietta Maylin. 19 1/2" by 14 1/2".
Chester County Historical Society collection.

Water color "Painted by Henrietta Maylin Autumn Fruit And Presented to Jacob Howell." 12 1/2″ by 12 1/2″.
Chester County Historical Society collection

Water color "Painted by Henrietta Maylin for her Friend Lizzie
Howell". 15″ by 12″.
Chester County Historical Society collection.

MURALS

Murals of the Baptist Church and minister's house in Parkesburg, attributed to Nuaugtus Neynabor who died in Honeybrook township in 1887. His work includes oil pictures, banners, lids of miniature chests, birth, marriage and death certificates. His work is found in both Chester and Lancaster counties.

William Penn Memorial Museum

T. E. Barrett

In 1844 T. E. Barrett advertised:

T. E. BARRETT,

Miniature Painter, from 136 Chestnut street, Philadelphia, BEGS leave respectfully to announce to the citizens of West Chester, that he purposes remaining a few days, and will be happy to wait on those who may desire his services in the line of his profession. His rooms are at the Chester County Hotel.[1]

E. C. Bisbee

In 1830 E. C. Bisbee advertised:

Portrait & Miniature Painting. E. C. BISBEE, respectfully informs the ladies and gentlemen of West-Chester and its vicinity, that he will offer them his services, in the above line of business in the course of a few days, or as soon as present engagements will permit. From his long experience and flattering encouragement he has uniformly had, he has confidence in assuring the public, that the permanency of his colors, the faithful and correct delineation of the features will secure his claims to public patronage. A number of specimens of his painting, in portrait and miniature, will be exhibited to the public.[2]

In 1848 he advertised:

PORTRAIT PAINTING. Mr. E. Bisbee, RESPECTFULLY informs the public of West Chester and its vicinity that he has taken rooms in the building occupied by Mrs. Matlack, in CHURCH street, where he will be prepared to paint portraits of large and small sizes, and copy Daguerreotypes in permanent oil colors.

Mr. B's long experience uniform success in the truthfulness of likenesses, and last though not least his very moderate charges, will offer all inducements to embrace the present opportunity of securing faithful likenesses of themselves and friends.

A few beautiful Cabinet portraits of Washington, copies from the original by G. Stuart, for sale. These have been universally admired and liberally patronized. Flags, Banners, and Transparencies, &c. executed in the best style. Pictures of every description cleaned, varnished and repaired.

N. B. Mr. B., will extend his practice to the country without extra charge.[3]

C. Burton

In 1835 C. Burton advertises:

Striking Likenesses,

C. BURTON

Professor of Perspective, and Drawing in General,

Oil painting by George Cope (born 1855, died 1929).
Chester County Historical Society collection

No. 13, Everhart's Hotel, grateful for the favors he has already received, respectfully informs the citizens of West Chester, that he proposes to remain here a few days longer, and is prepared to take
Truly Correct Portraits,
In a new and pleasing style, with black lead pencil, having the exact effect of a Lithographic print, and rendered durable by a chemical wash. Size 12 by 10 inches, at the moderate price of Three Dollars each. Ladies waited on at their residences. Specimens can be seen.

The Profile is the usual manner of taking the above Likeness, and is the most durable resemblance; as a person growing stouter or thinner will not alter the side face as it does the full face; yet the full or three quarter face can be taken, if desired, at an additional charge of One Dollar each.

As the above style of Portraits solely depends on the Expression of the Features, and has no color in it to deceive, to flatter, or to fade, so, also, a change of complexion cannot render it unlike, as is often the case with painted Likenesses. Need it be added that the separation of friends or relations, by death, marriage, removal, &c. often renders a Likeness not only desirable, but highly valuable.

C.B. is so successful in the practice, that he does not desire any one to take a Portrait, when done, if it is not known, as such, by two-thirds of his friends or neighbors.

Landscapes and Residences correctly drawn.[4]

C. Burton

Drawing Academy.

C. BURTON, professor of perspective, and drawing in general: being now engaged to give instruction in the Fine Arts, at Mr. Bolmar's Academy, has, (with his family) become a resident of West Chester; having located himself in Susan Webb's house, near the Cross Keys, Gay street and will be happy to fill up his time by receiving scholars at his residence, twice a week, at $8 per quarter; where every exertion will be made to advance the pupils, by scientific instruction, and occasional lectures on the art of perspective. C. B. also continues to take
Striking Likenesses,
with black lead pencil; size, 12 by 10 inches, at the moderate price of $3 each, or $5 for a man and his wife. Specimens of which may be seen in many parts of this town, as, also by calling above.

Transparent window blinds, painted on muslin, at from 10 to 20 dollars per pair; likewise scientific diagrams, painted on glass, with magic lanterns; for lectures on Astronomy, Botany, Optics, &c. &c.[5]

Mr. Crierson

In 1833 Mr. Crierson advertised:

MR. CRIERSON. PORTRAIT-PAINTER, RESPECTFULLY informs the ladies and gentlemen of this vicinity, that he will remain in Waynesburg a few weeks, and is prepared to take LIKENESSES at his room, at Mr. Pearson's tavern, on the most reasonable terms from $5 to $30. From long experience in his profession he feels assured he can render full satisfaction to those who may employ him. He invites the public to call and examine a few specimens of his workmanship.[6]

Oil painting by Caleb Fitzsimmons. 18″ by 24″.

Mr. and Mrs. Harold C. Fitzsimmons collection

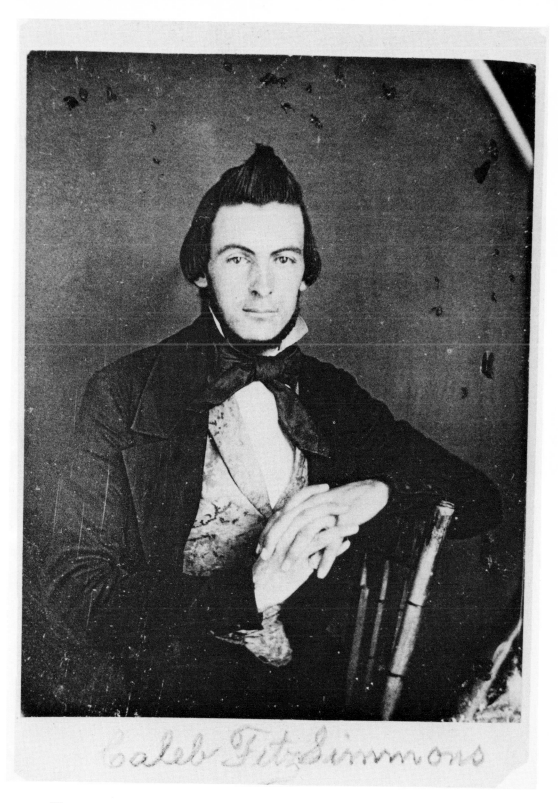

Photograph of Caleb Fitzsimmons.
Mr. and Mrs. Harold C. Fitzsimmons collection

Oil still life by Caleb Fitzsimmons. Born June 12, 1826; died August 24, 1856. 8″ by 12″.

Mr. and Mrs. Harold C. Fitzsimmons collection

Oil painting by Caleb Fitzsimmons. 25 3/4″ by 22″.
Mr. and Mrs. Harold C. Fitzsimmons collection

Oil portrait of Sarah James by John F. Francis. 29 1/2″ by 24 1/2″.
Chester County Historical Society collection

Mr. Dellawater

In 1846 a newspaper mentions:

Mr. DELLAWATER, Portrait Painter over Mr. Lewis' Office.
Mr. Editor:

Allow me in this manner to call the public attention and encouragement to Mr. Dellawater, a gentleman who has been but a short time in our Borough, and who has evinced talent in Portrait painting superior to any artist, (and we detract from none) that has ever been in the place. He has succeeded in giving to his pictures, the expression and spirit of the countenance with life like accuracy — he has caught it in its every-day every-where look, not as though it were studied and starched and fixed for the occasion—not a daub; not a caricature, not a flat outline— but raised and relieved from the canvass with fulness of form, every lineament and every proportion and every tint true to nature — representing not a corpse not a statue, but flesh and blood, living and breathing, with intelligence in the eyes, and language on the lips. And if we examine more critically, we shall find the judicious blending of colors, the happy disposition of light and shade, and the delicate finish equally admirable as the exactness and truth of the likeness — all evincing an artist of taste to appreciate and execute the beauties of his art; who has not wasted his days on speculative books, nor cramped his genius by hackneyed precepts nor been deluded by the prejudice of school and critics, but has studied life and form and color, as they are around him and about him, and learned from originals how "to hold the mirror up to nature."

PHILO — CROMO. [7]

Mr. Fletcher

A newspaper mentions in 1843:

AN EXHIBITION OF PAINTINGS,

Will we understand be held in the second story of The Cabinet, during next and the succeeding week.

The Paintings have been designed and executed by MR. FLETCHER, a young artist of talent and taste, who has been residing in our Borough, for several months, during which time he has taken excellent portraits of several of our citizens.

Mr. Fletcher is a native of our State, we believe, and the Paintings to be exhibited are, so far as we are capable of judging, highly creditable to him as an Artist, and deserving of patronage.

The exhibition will be open from 10 to 12, — from 2 to 4, and 7 to 9 o'clock, of each day. Admittance 25 cts. [8]

John F. Francis

The newspapers mention in 1848:

FINE ARTS.

JOHN F. FRANCIS respectfully informs the citizens of West Chester and the surrounding country, that he has opened a studio for Portrait Painting, a few doors east of the Mansion House, over Joseph J. Lewis's office. He respectfully invites the attention of the public and the ladies in particular, to his FREE Exhibition of Paintings, which will be open for a short time. . . [9]

PAINTINGS. – Mr. FRANCIS, who has his studio in this borough, over the office of J. J. Lewis, Esq. is an artist of rare excellence. We bespeak for him a liberal patronage. He has permanently located himself among us, and our county may feel proud of such an acquisition. – His portraits are to the life and many of his groupings of various figures, are in the highest style of delineation and perspective. We called in a few days ago and found much to gratify the eye. Mr. Francis will be pleased to have ladies and gentlemen to call and examine his specimens. They cannot fail to find the visit a pleasant one.[10]

John Langendoerffer

West-Chester 21st Oct. 1836.

Mr. David Townsend dr
To Th. Langendoerffer, Portrait painter,Cr

For a portrait	$ 16.00
For framing and frames	12.00
Box	2.00
	$ 30.00

Received the amount of the above Bill in full. West-Chester October 22d 1836.

SS LANGENDOERFFER[11]

Samuel Moon

Downingtown Oct 27th 1829

Dear Uncle

Some time past, I heard thy Daughter Phebe Haines and some of her Daughters, express a wish to have thy Portrait —— If thee is disposed to gratify them, there is a favourable opportunity at this time. Young Samuel Moon is in this neighbourhood takeing some for some of my neighbours, he is a young man of considerable merit, is a natural genius, and I think it necessary to have thine taken but thought that I would inform thee that Moon was here and if thee should think it worth while to have thine, and to favour him with a job my trouble would richly repaid, —if the should conclude to have it taken, please drop me a line, stating the time it will suit thee to come up and he will be ready to wait on thee —— His prices is, fifteen Dollars for full or life size twelve Dollars for the next below and ten for the smaller size —— miniature size is from five to ten Dollars. His prices are Moderate if the article was a real necessary one I remain thine &c

William W Downing

Richard Thomas Esq[12]

(Letter addressed: Richard Thomas Esq
West Whiteland
Township)   [13]

Oil portrait of Francis James by John F. Francis, an itinerant painter born in Montgomeryville. 29 1/2″ by 24 1/2″.

Chester County Historical Society collection

Oil portrait of Mary Ingram marked on the back "Vernon Fletcher Pinxt Westchester Pa Aug 1843 No 2". 30″ by 25 1/2″.

Mrs. and Mr. Harold C. Fitzsimmons collection

M. Moulthrop

In 1830 Mr. M. Moulthrop advertised:

NEW AND IMPROVED STYLE OF PAINTING FROM NATURE.
MR. M. MOULTHROP,

TEACHER of the imitation of Chinese Japanning, and Painting on Paper, respectfully informs the inhabitants of West-Chester, that he has taken Dr. BARBER'S Lecture Room in the Court-House, for the purpose of Exhibiting a collection of Specimens of his Painting; also the imitation of Japanning. Among this collection are several beautiful pieces, by pupils who had not any previous knowledge of the art.

The room will be open for the reception of Ladies and Gentlemen, on the 1st and 2d of December, inst. when his Paintings will be exhibited, and further particulars made known. Admission gratis. [14]

A week later a newspaper mentioned:

The PAINTINGS exhibited at the Court-House by Mr. Moulthrop, are spoken of by those who saw them, as remarkable for beauty; and many of them, the fruits particularly, for their accurate resemblance, were said by several "to make the mouth water, by the deliciousness of their appearance." [15]

Bass Otis

Westchester Novr 12th 1832

Mr. Lounes Taylor to B Otis Dr.
To Painting five portraits in bill
Sixty Dollars $ 60.00

Received payment in full

Bass Otis

John P. Sherwood

In 1831 John P. Sherwood advertised:

A CARD,

JOHN P. SHERWOOD, Portrait Painter, offers his services to the citizens of Chester county, for the execution of all business in his line, he hopes by strict attention and punctuality to whatever may be entrusted to him, to merit a share of public patronage. His charges will be moderate, and in no case will any compensation be required unless where satisfaction is given. He can always be found at Major Buckwalter's (Turk's Head,) or at his room in the West-Chester Academy. [16]

Later in the same year a newspaper mentions:

Mr. Sherwood, to whom I allude, is a young man, who is portrait and historical painter of great promise; he prosecutes the art with enthusiastic zeal; and I have had an opportunity of knowing that in more than one instance he has been so happy in his efforts, that his pictures would have done no discredit to the celebrated Stuart himself. [17]

Esther Strode

In 1831 newspapers mention:

A friend called on me the other day to take a ride to Strode's; the distance was not far — the day fine; the carriage at the door, and as the company pleased me well, I stepped in and away we drove. — The Cottage farm lay off to our right — the green hedge — the Nursery of Mulberries; the peach orchard; the willows beginning to assume the air of maturity, beautifully graceful like a young girl half advanced through her teens. Many day's of delightful labor had I expended there, and I could not pass it without a sigh, for I loved it well. To the left below, we passed the ancient mansion of a venerable friend — a charming plantation, highly cultivated and richly productive. The view brought to mind many pleasant recollections. Presently the mansion of a neighbor a little further on, came in sight — the fine meadows — luxuriant grape vines — the neat barn and superior garden — the whole a pattern of excellent farming. Strode's Mill, and the mansion house came next. — We alighted for the purpose of our visit, to see the paintings of Miss ESTHER STRODE. This young lady having discovered a talent for portrait painting, was induced, by the advice of her friends, to spend some time in Philadelphia under the tuition of NAGLE, the celebrated artist, to improve herself in painting. She has recently returned home and now takes the portraits of those who may favor her with their patronage. Without pretending to be connoisseurs in the difficult art, we have yet an eye keenly sensitive to what appears to be beauties & defects. In examining numerous productions of Miss Strode's pencil, we confess ourselves to have been much gratified. To us she seems to possess genius, taste and skill. While the painting is beautifully pleasing to the eye her pictures have a higher merit — indeed the chief merit of portraits, that without which no beauty of coloring, no disposition of light and shade — no gracefulness of drapery, can avail — her portraits are striking likenesses. Several seemed natural enough to speak to us. — We do

not mean to praise — but merely to bear justice to merit.

Those who are desirous of procuring likenesses of themselves or friends — the wealthy and liberal who wish to promote the fine arts in Chester county, and to encourage native genius, we would recommend to call and see Miss Strode's paintings. [18]

Availing ourselves of the opportunity, we visited with great pleasure, a collection of paintings, consisting of portraits, landscapes, &c. from the classical pencil of Miss Esther Strode. As an artist, we may safely say, Miss S. promises to become a brilliant ornament to our county. To the possession of superior native talents, she has added the highest cultivation. She studies with much reputation under Nagle, the celebrated portrait painter of Philadelphia, and it is no detriment to that eminent artist, to assert that the pupil is worthy of her distinguished tutor. Miss Strode possesses a peculiar and delicate richness in her style of painting, which we have seldom seen equalled — and her likenesses are true as nature's self. We would recommend any of our friends, who desire to see themselves seated upon canvass with the wondrous accuracy of breathing humanity, to call on Miss Strode, and if they are not pleased with their picture, it may be taken for granted they cannot view their own image with complacency. [19]

Oil portrait by John Landendoeffer of David Townsend. Painted in
1836. 25 1/2″ by 31 1/4″.

Chester County Historical Society collection

Mr. Williams

In 1840 a newspaper mentions:

Mr. Williams — The Artist.

This gentleman has had a place among us for nearly two years, during which time he has exhibited numerous evidences of skill and proficiency in his profession, which cannot have failed being observed by all who have visited his gallery of paintings and inspected the various offsprings of his genius and art. Though young in years, we venture to say our county can boast of not many who can equal, and but few who can excel him in inscribing upon canvass the features and expressions of the human face. More striking and correct portraits, than those which proceed from his hand, are seldom produced by our most famed painters. Practice, study, and observation will ere long, place him by the side of those who rank highest in his profession.

We regret to learn that Mr. Williams contemplates taking leave of our borough, in the course of a few weeks;—say about the middle of March. It would be advisable, therefore, for those who wish to avail themselves of his services, to give him a call at an early day; and it is his desire that all his patrons who have not yet removed their portraits, will do so, previous to his departure. [20]

Wm. Winner

In 1837 Wm. Winner advertised:

WM WINNER, Portrait Painter, RESPECTFULLY gives notice to the inhabitants of West Chester and vicinity, that his stay here is limited to four weeks from this date. Those persons wishing their likenesses, either in large or miniature, will please call early, in the Cabinet, room No. 5, 2nd story. [21]

[1] *Village Record,* (West Chester, Pa.), Dec. 6, 1837.

[2] *Jeffersonian,* (West Chester, Pa.), Feb. 27, 1844.

[3] *Village Record,* (West Chester, Pa.), March 17, 1830.

[4] *Jeffersonian,* (West Chester, Pa.), Nov. 1, 1848.

[5] *Village Record,* (West Chester, Pa.), Sept. 9, 1835.

[6] Ibid., Dec. 2, 1835.

[7] *Waynesburg Press,* (Honey Brook, Pa.), Oct. 25, 1833.

[8] *Village Record,* (West Chester, Pa.), Sept. 1, 1846.

[9] *American Republican,* (West Chester, Pa.), Dec. 19, 1843.

[10] *Register & Examiner,* (West Chester, Pa.), April 18, 1848.

[11] *Village Record,* (West Chester, Pa.), April 25, 1848.

[12] *Chester County Historical collection*

[13] *Chester County Historical collection*

Oil still life by George Cope (born 1855, died 1929). Signed in left corner "GeoCope 09". Picture was painted for "Mr. Wilmer J. Nields Chatham Chester County Pa". 23″ by 19″.
Chester County Historical Society collection

[14]*Chester County Historical Society collection*

[15]*Village Record,* (West Chester, Pa.), Dec. 1, 1830.

[16]Ibid., (West Chester, Pa.), Dec. 8, 1830.

[17]*Village Record,* (West Chester, Pa.), March 9, 1831.

[18]*American Republican,* (West Chester, Pa.), no date, 1831.

[19]*Village Record,* (West Chester, Pa.), Aug. 24, 1831.

[20]*American Republican,* (West Chester, Pa.), Oct. 4, 1831.

[21]*American Republican,* (West Chester, Pa.), Feb. 18, 1840.

Oil portrait by Bass Otis of Rebecca Webb Baker, wife of Lownes
Taylor. Painted in 1832. 36 1/2″ by 63 3/4″.

Chester County Historical Society collection

Oil painting by Bass Otis of the Lownes Taylor farm in Goshen Township. Painted in 1832. 40 1/4″ by 52″.
Chester County Historical Society collection

Oil painting by Thomas Buchanan Reed (born 1822, died 1872).
Chester County Historical Society collection

Oil portrait attributed to Esther Strode of Jane (Pyle) Brinton. 30″ by 25 1/2″.

Mrs. Samuel A. McCain collection

Oil portrait attributed to Esther Strode of George Brinton. 28″ by 22 1/2″.

Mrs. Samuel A. McCain collection

Water color of the Court House by J. Bayard Taylor. Picture marked "Views of West Chester No. 1, Chester County Court House Sept. 1, 1840 J. B. Taylor". The Court House was erected in West Chester in 1786.
Chester County Historical Society collection

Water color of the prison in West Chester by J. Bayard Taylor ca. 1840. He was a prolific mid-nineteenth century author. (born 1825, died 1878)
Chester County Historical Society collection

Water Color of the Bank of Chester County by Bayard Taylor. The picture is marked "From Nature Sept. 3rd, 1840. J. B. Taylor Del". 8 1/2″ by 11 1/4″.

Chester County Historical Society collection

Oil portrait by Samuel Moon of Richard Thomas. 27″ by 24″.
Anonymous

Oil portraits of Jane and Robert Morris ca. 1753 attributed to Benjamin West who was born in Chester County in 1738. He went to England and became President of the Royal Academy in London. West died in 1820. 19 1/2″ by 19 1/2″.

Mrs. John E. Cornwell collection

Portraits of Francis and Sarah James, of West Chester. Attributed to
C. Burton. 13″ by 10″.

Chester County Historical Society collection

SIGNS

John Brown

John Brown, of West Chester, advertised in 1827:

. . .N.B. All kinds of repairing done in the best manner and for the most reduced prices. Carving for Cabinet Makers — Job and Sign Painting of all descriptions, neatly executed.

John Brown.[1]

John Dawney

John Dawney, of West Chester, advertised in 1845:

House, Sign Painting and GLAZING. The subscriber would respectfully inform his friends and the public generally, that he has located himself in New Street, a few doors north of Gay, near the public house of William Glover, where he is prepared to prosecute the above business in all its various branches. By a long practical experience in his line of business, he feels confident of giving general satisfaction to those who may favor him with their patronage. In short, by combining cheapness of charge with superior workmanship and style he is satisfied of being able to merit a reasonable share of public custom.

JOHN DAWNEY.[2]

R. F. Henderson

R. F. Henderson, of West Chester, advertised in 1845:

TO THE PUBLIC

R. F. HENDERSON informs the citizens of West Chester and vicinity, that he has opened a shop in High street, near the Black Bear tavern, for the purpose of carrying on his business. House, Sign, Ornamental PAINTING and GLAZING; also Paper Hanging, where punctual attendance will be given at the shortest notice. [3]

Three years later he advertised:

Take Notice.

THE subscriber hereby tenders his thanks to the people of the borough and its vacinity for the liberal patronage he has received, and respectfully solicits the continuation of their favors. He considers himself completely master of his profession in all its various branches, having had eighteen years of experience in House and Sign Painting and Glazing; also Wall Painting and Paper Hanging, Imitation of Woods, Marble and Ground Glass. He has also a material that he will warrant not to rub off on the outside, which he has found out by experience. All orders promptly attended to. Shop on the south side of Market street, opposite to the Market House.

R. F. HENDERSON[4]

Sign for the Turk's Head Tavern.
43″ by 37 1/2″.
Chester County Historical Society collection

Matthew Jackson

The will of Matthew Jackson, of West Chester, proven in 1846 mentions that he was a sign painter.[5] His good will was bought by John P. Rawlings.

Andrew Kilpatrick

Andrew Kilpatrick, of West Chester, advertised in 1844:

ANDREW KILPATRICK, successor to Angus McKay, House, Sign & Ornamental Painter and Glazier, Market street, West Chester, three doors east of the Methodist Church, where he will be pleased to receive a share of public patronage.

Sign and Ornamental Painting, Gilding, Bronzing, Graining, Transferring, Paper Hanging &c., executed with neatness and despatch.[6]

Angus M'Kay

Angus M'Kay, of West Chester, advertised in 1830:

HOUSE AND SIGN PAINTING, AND GLAZING. THE subscriber returns his thanks to his friends and the public, for the liberal encouragement he has received from them, and hopes by prompt attention to his business, to merit a continuance of their favors. Those who wish to have painting done, are assured that the best materials shall always be used, and the work done in a durable and workmanlike manner, by applying to the subscriber, fourth dwelling-house in Ogden's new row, Gay-Street.

ANGUS M'KAY

In 1830 and 1831 he advertised for an apprentice.[7]

John P. Rawlings

John P. Rawlings, of West Chester, advertised in 1846:

JOHN P. RAWLINGS, from Phila. House and Sign Painter and Glazier. HAVING bought out the good will, &c. of Matthew Jackson, and the said Matthew Jackson having signed over to me all his customers' work, I feel myself competent to do all kinds of House, Sign and Wall Painting, Wall Coloring, Imitation of Woods and Marbles, Gilding, Bronzing, Paper Hanging, &c.

Having long done work in Philadelphia, for the Friends in Arch street.[8]

The following year he advertised:

. . .that he is prepared to do House Painting either by the lump, or by the day, by the pound, or any way convenient for those who may wish work done; . . .

Where persons find their own paint, he will furnish pot and brushes for $1 17; as I have to pay $1 50 per day myself, and I find brushes. I employ none but good workmen — those who have served a regular apprenticeship to the business — any others I will not have.

Old and new Glazing done at reasonable rate.

Ready-mixed Paint of all colors, to be had, and warranted to dry in a few hours.

J. P. RAWLINGS.[9]

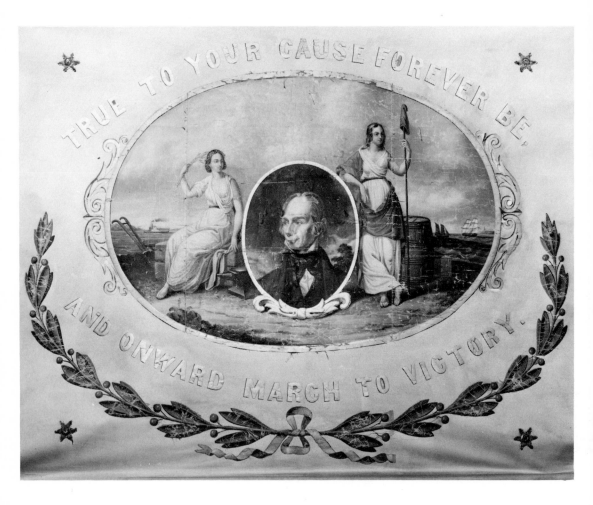

Banner
46″ by 40 1/2″.
Chester County Historical Society collection

In 1848 he advertised:

SLOW AND SURE.

Cheap. . .Cheapest, in this place.

HOUSE & SIGN PAINTING & GLAZING done 25 per cent lower than ever. Call, see and judge for yourself. I can work for any price or any way — by the job or measurements.

Sign work from 8 cts per foot to 37 1/2 cents. Gilt Sign from 25 to 50 cents.

For plain Painting, one coat white, by square yd., 6 cents; two coats 9 cents, three coats 12 1/2, where there is a quantity to do. Higher price colors in proportion.

Old Glazing 8 by 10 and Glass, all over one dozen lights will be done per light at 9 to 10 cents.

10 by 12 and glass	12 to 14
10 by 14 and glass	16 to 20
10 by 16 and glass	20 to 25

New Glazing and Painting sash, two coats,

8 by 10	6 cts per light
10 by 12	10 cts per light
10 by 14	14 cts per light

The materials shall be of the best.

J. P. RAWLINGS.[10]

Daniel Scotten

Daniel Scotten, of West Chester, advertised in 1845:

HOUSE AND SIGN PAINTING, PAPER-HANGING, &C. THE Subscriber respectfully informs his friends and the public in general, that he is prepared to execute in a workmanlike manner, any job that may be entrusted to him in the above line of business. Thankful for past favors, he trusts that he will receive the patronage which strict attention to business, and the excellence and durability of his work may merit. He will use every exertion to give satisfaction to all who may employ him, and his charges will be moderate. Parlor blinds painted and trimmed, and at a short notice. — His shop is at the corner of Church and Chestnut Streets, just above the late residence of Milton Early, Coach-maker.

DANIEL SCOTTEN.[11]

William Wickersham

William Wickersham, of West Chester, advertised in 1830:

WM. WICKERSHAM,
HOUSE PAINTER, GLAZIER, PAPER
HANGER AND SIGN PAINTER

RESPECTFULLY informs his friends and the public in general that he continues to carry on the above business, in all its various branches, IN THE BOROUGH OF W. CHESTER, and its surrounding neighborhood, he intends going both far and near to accommodate those, who may give him a call in his line of business, together with modest

Banner
51 1/2″ by 39″.
Chester County Historical Society collection

charges and good workmanship, he hopes to merit a share of public patronage.

Country produce will be taken in exchange for work.

N.B. An apprentice wanted to the above business, a lad between the age of 15 and 18, of good moral habits would be preferred.[12]

[1]*Village Record,* (West Chester, Pa.), Feb. 14, 1827.

[2]*Jeffersonian,* (West Chester, Pa.), Feb. 4, 1845.

[3]*Village Record,* (West Chester, Pa.), Dec. 16, 1845.

[4]Ibid., April 11, 1848.

[5]*Chester County Will Book 19,* p. 99.

[6]*Village Record,* (West Chester, Pa.), Nov. 4, 1844.

[7]*Village Record,* (West Chester, Pa.), April 28, 1830.

[8]*Village Record,* (West Chester, Pa.), July 21, 1846.

[9]Ibid., June 1, 1847.

[10]Ibid., Aug. 29, 1848.

[11]*Register & Examiner,* (West Chester, Pa.), Oct. 28, 1845.

[12]*Village Record,* (West Chester, Pa.), Jan. 28, 1830.

Inn sign painted by John A. Woodside (born 1781, died 1852).
Chester County Historical Society collection

Stone

This fountain is described in a newspaper in 1869:

DRINKING FOUNTAIN IN WEST CHESTER.— We have been shown
the design for the Drinking Fountain, to be erected on High street,
in front of the Court House, in this Borough. It will be erected
close to the curb, about half-way between the corner of High and

Market streets and the gate leading into the Court House yard. Already an opening has been made in the pavement to receive it, and Messrs. Garrett & Jones, Marble Manufacturers, West Chester, are now busily at work upon it, and expect to complete it in a manner creditable to their establishment in about two weeks. It is being made from Chester county marble – dove color – from the quarries of the Messrs. Thomas Brothers, West Whiteland. The design gotten up by Rev. John Bolton, is to represent Rock-Work; it will have a basin facing the pavement for the use of individuals, and on the side fronting the street there will be a trough for watering horses, immediately beneath which and close to the ground will be another basin or trough, at which thirsty and panting "Carlo" and other members of the canine family can stop and quench their thirst. The whole will be surmounted by a neat ornament, and when complete will be about eight feet in height, and will cost in the neighborhood of $350. The inscriptions have not yet been decided on. The idea of erecting a public fountain in West Chester originated with Mrs. John Hickman, who had been kindly assisted in the laudable work by other ladies of our Borough, all of whom are certainly entitled to much praise, and they will no doubt receive the heart-felt thanks of many a weary traveler as he refreshes himself with a cold drink of water. Aside from its usefulness it will be a pretty ornament to our town.

Since the above was put in type we understand the following will be put on the fountain.

> Thirsty traveler, see in Me
> An emblem of true charity;
>   My life I give,
>   That you may live—
> And I've a fresh supply from Heaven,[1]
> For every cup of water given.

In 1879 a newspaper mentions:

ALTERING THE FOUNTAIN.– The cross and circle that formerly adorned the top of the fountain in front of the Court House became broken last winter from some cause. Workmen are engaged in placing upon it a round urn.[2]

In 1881:

Broke the Fountain.– A young lad who was playing in front of the Court House last evening about 7 o'clock got upon the fountain and accidentally pulled the top off and broke the marble ball, both the boy and the ball falling to the ground together.[3]

In 1882:

Major D. Jones, marble cutter, has been making some improvements to the marble fountain in front of the Court House, which have been completed, and the fountain is now being re-erected.[4]

In 1960:

A land mark is missing from in front of the county Court House in West Chester. Last week the marble drinking fountain for horses, on the west side of the street, near High, was finally moved. It is now on the grounds of the Townsend House on N. Matlack St. There it will ultimately become an ornamental addition to the formal garden which lies behind the historic home. The fountain stood on High St. since 1860. It had been about 50 years, however, since it was used for its original purpose of watering horses. As a matter of fact its supply of water had been cut off for more than a quarter of a century. About the only incident attendant upon its removal was the finding of an 1800 penny by the workmen filling in the hole from the base of the fountain was removed. For what it is worth, Old Ed was told, the penny too, was turned over to the Chester County Historical Society.[5]

On January 16, 1810 the *American Republican,* in West Chester mentions:

STONE CUTTING

THE subscriber returns his sincere thanks to his friends and customers and the public in general, for past favors, — and begs to inform them that he has on hand, several Tombs, Head and Foot Stones, Chimney Pieces, Hearths, Door-sills and Paint Stones — all of which he will sell at reduced prices for Cash or Barter, as he will decline said business in Downingtown, by the first of April, ensuing.

FREDERICK SYFRIT.

Jan. 16, 1810
N.B. A suitable Stone for a Currying Table may be had.

The 1850 Census return mentions:

George W. Shafer (prob) 37 years, marble sculptor, Phoenixville B.Pa.
Stephen Blatchford 51 years marble mason, E. Caln B. England.

The *Village Record,* in West Chester, on July 20, 1869 mentions:

Beautiful Work of Art . . . to a beautiful piece of Statuary, the work of Mr. Julius E. Beck, Professor of Drawing and Penmanship, at Mr. Wyers' Academy in the Borough. The subject of this work is the figure of a sleeping child, executed in fine American Statuary Marble. The figure that of a babe, eleven months old, is 28 inches long (life size) and rests upon a cushion partly covered with drapery, which hangs over the sides. It is intended to be placed over the grave of a little child. . .

The *Daily Local News, in West Chester, on April 2, 1873* mentions:

HANDSOME TOMBSTONE

Mr. David Jones' marble Yard, a handsomely wrought stone destined to commemorate the resting-place of Daniel Nields, dec'd. This tribute is of Italian marble, resting on an American marble vase. It is about five feet high with oval top. . .

[1] *Village Record,* (West Chester, Penna.), July 27, 1869.

[2] *Daily Local News,* (West Chester, Penna.), July 2, 1879.

[3] Ibid., May 28, 1881.

[4] Ibid., May 20, 1882.

[5] Ibid., Oct. 10, 1960.

1748 Tombstone of Jane Hathorn. By tradition she departed this life at the age of 94 while reaching for the four of diamonds.

Graveyard at Lewisville, Elk township

1742 Tombstone inscribed: In/ Memory of/ Peter Bezellon/ Who departed this Life/ July the 18th 1742/ Aged 80 years/ Who ere shold with tender Heart/ Stop Read & think on Me/ I once was well as now thou art/ As now I am so thou shalt be

St. John's Church, Compassville, West Caln township

Date stone, Collins Mansion, West Goshen Township, 1727.

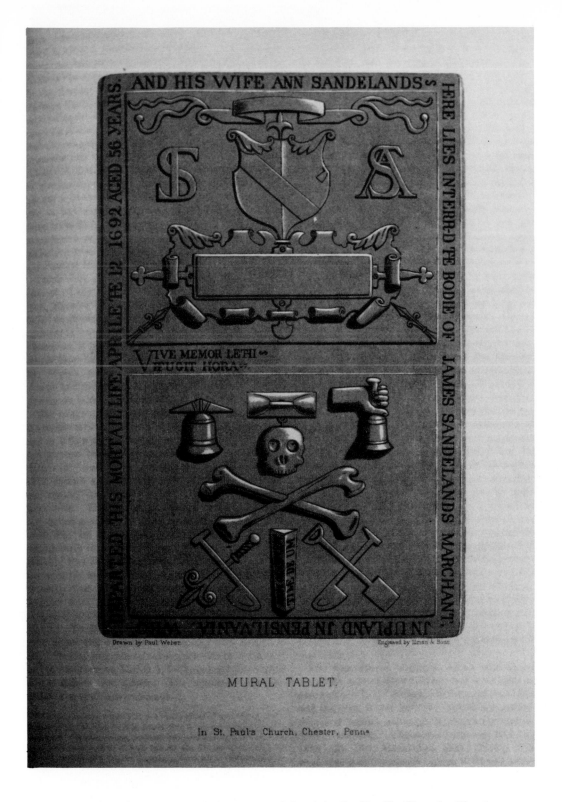

1692 Mural tablet of James Sandeland in St. Paul's Church, Chester, Pa. *History of Delaware County, Pennsylvania* by Henry Graham Ashmead, (Phila., L. W. Everts & Co. 1884), p. 338.

Marble Bust of William Darlington M.D. by William Marshall Swayne who was born in Pennsbury township December 1, 1828 and died in Kennett Square on May 8, 1918. He was a self-taught sculptor who obtained sittings from some of the most prominent men of his time. Height 29″.

Chester County Historical Society collection

Marble Bust of General Anthony Wayne by William Marshall Swayne.
Chester County Historical Society collection

Hair Wreath.
Chester County Historical Society collection

Sundries

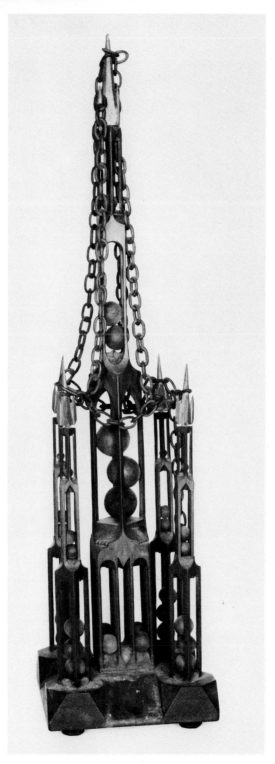

Carved wood folly made by John B. Temple. Height 33″. Carved out of one piece of wood.

Chester County Historical Society collection

Wayne homestead, Easttown township. Carved in wood. First section of the house built in 1742. 18 1/4″ by 15 3/4″.

Titus C. Geesey collection

Feather Wreath.
Chester County Historical Society collection

Shell vase and flowers.
Chester County Historical Society collection

Paper lamp shade marked in cross stitch "Married 3d mo 6th 1873 Froom J E Bride BSC". Height 6 3/4″, diameter at bottom 26″.

Chester County Historical Society collection

Quillwork picture. Signed on the back "Made by Sarah Boehme Westchester in Pennsylvania" ca. 1830.

Chester County Historical Society collection

Mid-eighteenth century shell and wax works.

Chester County Historical Society collection